The
Leader's Way

HIS HOLINESS THE

DALAI LAMA

and LAURENS VAN DEN MUYZENBERG

The

[Leader's Way]

The Art of Making the Right Decisions

in Our Careers, Our Companies,

and the World at Large

BROADWAY BOOKS

New York

Published in the United States by Broadway Books, an imprint of the
Crown Publishing Group, a division of Random House, Inc., New York.
www.broadwaybooks.com

First published in Great Britain and the Commonwealth by Nicholas
Brealey Publishing, London, in 2009. This edition published by
arrangement with Nicholas Brealey Publishing.

Library of Congress Cataloging-in-Publication Data
Bstan-'dzin-rgya-mtsho, Dalai Lama XIV, 1935–
The leader's way : the art of making the right decisions in our careers,
our companies, and the world at large / His Holiness the Dalai Lama &
Laurens van den Muyzenberg. — 1st ed.
p. cm.
Includes bibliographical references and index.
1. Leadership. 2. Management. I. Muyzenberg, Laurens van den. II.
Title.
HD57.7.B795 2009
658.4'092—dc22
2008054645

ISBN 978-0-385-52780-4

PRINTED IN THE UNITED STATES OF AMERICA

10 9 8 7 6 5 4 3 2 1

First U.S. Edition

Contents

Introduction

His Holiness the Dalai Lama

Generally, Buddhist monks are somewhat isolated from the rest of society, often secluded in peace while praying for the welfare of all sentient beings and for our planet. Although I am one such monk, I also have responsibilities with regard to the Tibetan government-in-exile, which offers me a broader perspective in that I interact with people from all over the world. In the course of my travels I have met many different kinds of people, some of them poor, some of them rich, each of them occupying their own position in the world. People appear to trust me; therefore, many have talked to me about their lives, their hopes, and their concerns about the future. In the end, I have learned that what almost everyone is seeking is a measure of happiness.

Why am I writing this book now? Because I feel we all should have a sincere concern and responsibility for how the global economy operates and an interest in the role of businesses in shaping our interconnectedness. Times have changed, and I believe that leaders of religious traditions—with their ability to take a long view of the human condition—should participate in discussions of global business and economics. Our world faces very serious problems. Those that are of particular concern to me include the overwhelming degree of poverty in poor countries; the fact that even in prosperous countries the sense of satisfaction with life has been stagnating since 1950; the negative impact that our negligence and our ever-increasing population and rising standard of living are having on the environment; and finally, the lack of peace in so many parts of the world.

Because Buddhism takes a rational and logical attitude toward such problems, its approach is sometimes easier to understand for those who are not religious than for those who are. In Buddhism, there is an emphasis on human values and on how we can be taught to take a holistic approach to solving society's problems. So if we view Buddhist teachings in terms of secular ethics and fundamental human values, then perhaps they too have something to contribute to the business world.

Buddhist concepts about wealth, work, consumption, and happiness are somewhat different from their Western counterparts. Happiness is more than merely satisfying our material wishes and desires. The root of happiness is not in what we desire or what we get but somewhere altogether different. It stems from a place of inner contentment that exists no matter what we gain or achieve.

Buddha recognized that self-oriented drives were very powerful. However, he came to the conclusion that the drive to satisfy the desires of the self was impossible to achieve, a never-ending cycle. People cannot be truly happy unless they have friendships and good relationships with other people. Furthermore, good relationships are reciprocal. It is impossible for people to build positive relationships with others if their only aim is to satisfy their own desires. So I believe that governments and organizations, which bring people into contact with one another, as well as create jobs and wealth, have a very important role to play in these questions of the standard of living and human happiness—and where the two may intersect.

I do not pretend that the solutions to the world's problems are simple or straightforward. While working on this book, I have come to understand how difficult it can be for businesspeople to make the right decisions. When the leader of a company makes a decision, it affects all the employees and many others who buy the company's products or act as suppliers, and therefore the quality of business decisions is critical. This becomes especially complex for large, global corporations operating in many countries. For this reason, the decision maker not only must be competent, but must also have the right motivation and the right state of mind. Competence specific to business measures both talent and knowledge; as such, it is beyond the scope of this book. However, observing and correcting your motivation is an important aspect of Buddhist practice and is discussed in detail here, as is cultivating the right state of mind.

Fundamental to Buddhist philosophy is the notion that suffering exists and that the Buddha calls on all of us to help alleviate it. My aim in this book is the same: to enable readers and leaders to reduce suffering and increase satisfaction with life as a whole by helping them to understand more clearly what happens in their minds and the minds of others. As a consequence, this book will help leaders everywhere make good decisions that will generate a better quality of life for themselves, their organizations, and everyone else affected by those decisions.

————

My own interest and thinking about business and economics has evolved over the last fifty years. My formal training has been of an entirely religious and spiritual character; since my youth, my field of study has been Buddhist philosophy and psychology. To some extent, due to my interaction with Tibetan and Chinese members of the Communist Party, I gradually learned about different economic systems. By inclination, I found I first leaned toward socialism, but as I watched the economies in socialist countries stagnate while the free-market economies grew clearly more dynamic, I became particularly interested in what had gone wrong with the socialist economies and in the positive aspects of the free market (though I do remain concerned that the free-market system tends to increase the gap between the rich and the poor).

In 1990, I received a letter from Laurens van den Muyzenberg, an international management consultant. He suggested that rather than seeking to combine the common themes of communism and Buddhist thinking, as I had earlier envisaged, it would be more effective to consider how capitalism could be improved in an attempt to address our collective concerns. I found the idea appealing and asked him to visit me; we met many times over the intervening years. Then in 1999, Laurens suggested that given the increasing interest in governance among global companies—and the fact that the Buddhist tradition includes many theoretical and practical instructions that would be helpful to people in businesses, especially their leaders—I should be able to make a contribution to the literature on the subject. And thus, this book was born. We agreed at the outset that we wanted the book to be of practical use and to help businesspeople make better decisions. We decided that Laurens would describe the business issues and I would explain how to apply Buddhist teachings to the issues he raised.

I advised Laurens to take a holistic approach. By "holistic" I meant that he should look at issues from many different perspectives, not solely that of a management consultant from the West. I believe one of the main problems in the world today is that, while the amount of information is growing exponentially, people are becoming more and more narrow in their worldview and are no longer able to understand how all these ideas for improving society interact.

In writing this book, I selected subjects that I think are important and Laurens investigated them based on his own experience, discussion with professional colleagues, and research of published information. He also interviewed business leaders who were active Buddhist practitioners about the impact of Buddhism on their approach to business. We do not claim to have found all the answers, but we have taken pains to present Buddhist teachings in a useful way that businesspeople can easily understand.

I am not interested in converting readers of this book to Buddhism. My interest is to present Buddhist concepts in a way that is useful to people from all religious faiths, and even to those without any specific religious faith.

This book is not about Buddhism as a religion or as a way of life. I believe that people can find values to help them lead a good and responsible life in all religious traditions. I also believe that people who do not follow any religion can lead a good and responsible life. The ideas in this book are therefore possible for everyone to accept and practice.

I have faced a great many difficulties in my life. I lost my freedom at the age of sixteen and became a refugee at twenty-four.
Nevertheless, I can say that due to my Buddhist training, I am
happier than many people who take for granted freedom and a
country they call their own. This ability to maintain my peace of
mind is entirely due to the teachings I have received and my
consistent efforts to put them into practice by training my mind.
My sincere hope is that with this book, I can help our leaders—
in business and global organizations—learn and apply this same
training to bring about a more peaceful and sustainable planet.

The Monk and the Management Consultant

Laurens van den Muyzenberg

This project is about the meeting of two worlds: my world of management consulting, specifically the global marketplace, and the Dalai Lama's world of Tibetan Buddhism. It has been the most exciting and rewarding professional experience of my life.

After I read in one of His Holiness's books about an Indian philosopher who was working on a synthesis between communism and Buddhism, I wrote to His Holiness to say I thought it would be easier to make a synthesis between Buddhism and capitalism. Somewhat to my surprise, I received a letter from His Holiness inviting me to come and visit him in India. From 1991 to 2000, I met with the Dalai Lama every year and did small consulting projects for him, including seminars about strategy for his government-in-exile.

At the beginning, my knowledge of Buddhist teachings was limited; so too was the Dalai Lama's experience with economics and the world of business. Although His Holiness had studied the socialist system and the works of Karl Marx, his exposure to the free-market system was more limited. The idea was that I would brief the Dalai Lama on an economic area and His Holiness would comment on the issues based on his perspective.

These discussions covered many of the basics of business and as such had little to do with Buddhism. However, it soon became clear that the Dalai Lama wanted to understand and see the big picture—how business fits into society and the true meaning of "corporate responsibility." As His Holiness said, "I want a holistic perspective on business." After some seven years of meeting with each other, we had found a way to synthesize the concepts of Buddhism with those of prominent Western thinkers to cope better with the dilemmas of business. Hence, this book was born.

The world today faces many challenges. True, our total wealth has increased enormously and we are benefiting from technological miracles. But at the same time, billions of people are living in abject poverty, we face the imminent threat of environmental disaster, and even those in prosperous nations feel insecure about the future. Addressing these problems requires a different kind of leadership, one that sees things as they really are and seeks to resolve them in a holistic way. That is what this book is about.

True leaders have the ability to look at an issue from many perspectives and, based on that expanded view, make the right decisions. They have a calm, collected, and concentrated mind, undisturbed by negative thoughts and emotions, trained and focused. And true leadership recognizes the inevitability of change, the need for a sense of universal responsibility, and the importance of combining an economic system with moral values. That is the leader's way.

The book is structured progressively: starting with the

individual, leading to the company or organization, and culminating with society at large. Remember, authentic leaders and change makers are not exclusively found among top management, and we encourage employees at all levels to find their leader within by employing the practices in this book.

Part 1, "Leading Yourself," discusses the basics of Buddhism and how the teachings of the Buddha apply in all aspects of life. We emphasize the importance of good decision making, as well as the development of mental exercises that improve the performance of the mind. We also introduce some of the fundamental concepts of Buddhism.

In part 2, "Leading Your Organization," we take the ideas and principles of part I and show how they can be applied in the business framework. Here, leaders of organizations are encouraged to bring warmth, compassion, integrity, and ethics into their decision making and their policies and procedures; in their turn, companies are encouraged to look for leaders with integrity.

Part 3, "Leading in an Interconnected World," then seeks to apply Buddhist values on a global scale. Here we address the important topics of poverty, sustainability, diversity, and environmental responsibility. We believe that by making even small changes in their approach to these issues, today's leaders can foster hope and the possibility of a better world.

And this is the ultimate wish of the Dalai Lama—and me: that by improving the quality of our leaders' decisions, we will find ourselves in a better world for everyone.

Part 1

[Leading Yourself]

The best way for a ruler to reign over his country

is first of all to rule himself.

I

Taking the Right View

Some people have the mistaken impression that Buddhism leads only to passivity, to people forsaking this materialistic world and meditating in the forest. In truth, this kind of isolation is intended primarily for monks and nuns. As a philosophy, Buddhism does deal with classic philosophical questions: What is truth and how can we ascertain it? What is the purpose of life? What is this universe in which we dwell? What are human nature, duty, and destiny? What is good and what is bad?

But the main emphasis of Buddhism is specifically on taking the right actions: what should I do? The essence of Buddhism can be summed up in the two concepts of Right View and Right Conduct. The Right View is of no value if it does not lead to the Right Action—and taking the right action is obviously fundamental for the success of business. As Laurens explains:

> *Leadership is about making decisions, and not just any decisions—the right ones. Leaders of global companies*

make decisions that affect thousands or even millions of people, and political leaders make decisions that affect tens or hundreds of millions. Therefore, making the wrong decisions can have disastrous effects. The purpose of this chapter is to show how leaders can improve the quality of the decisions they make by applying some central concepts of Buddhist philosophy to improve their minds.

The Buddhist view is that a true leader is one who makes the right decisions. And making the right decisions depends on taking the Right View, which leads to the Right Action. Taking the Right View involves what the Dalai Lama refers to as "a calm, collected, and concentrated mind," one that is peaceful, undisturbed by negative thoughts and emotions, trained, and focused. It is a central concept of Buddhism that every man and every woman can decide to improve his or her mind, and that doing so will lead to a happier life for himself or herself and others. You can improve your mind by thinking the right way and acting the right way. But you cannot improve your mind if you do not think *the right way.*

Thinking the right way means making sure that every action is based on the right intention and the right motivation. The right intention is that the action will be beneficial to you and everyone affected by it; that is, it takes into account the well-being of the self and others. This is true for individuals and for organizations.

Having the right intention is the first part of the Buddhist concept of Right View. The second part recognizes three aspects of reality: impermanence, interdependence, and dependent origination. Buddhism teaches that nothing exists that is permanent; nothing exists that is independent; and nothing exists without a cause. You may think that this is rather obvious, but all too often people forget to take it into account when making decisions.

Recognizing interdependence and continuous change is also the basis of systems thinking in the West. Many prominent contributions to this field have been made by academics at the Massachusetts Institute of Technology— for example, Peter Senge in organizational learning, Jay Forrester in systems dynamics, and Marvin Minsky's Society of Mind theory of human cognition. The Santa Fe Institute in New Mexico, with its many Nobel Prize winners, such as Murray Gell-Mann and Kenneth Arrow, continues to advance knowledge on how a complex system like the economy, even society, functions. They all seek to answer many of the same questions as Buddhism. How do causes and effects interact? In other words, like Buddhists, systems thinkers take a "holistic" view of society and the world.

Thinking the right way depends on having a calm, collected, and concentrated mind. If your mind is influenced by anger, jealousy, fear, or lack of self-confidence, you become disturbed and inefficient; you cannot see reality; and your mind is no longer calm, collected, and concentrated. To achieve the Right View, you have to develop the capability of mindfulness. Mindfulness means that you can see when a negative emotion starts to influence your mind. You also have to develop the ability to stop these negative emotions from taking control over your mind. In other words, you have to gain and maintain control over the state of your mind to make your decisions according to Right View. In the next few chapters we explain how to train your mind in this way.

While Right View relates to the intention behind a decision, Right Conduct, another Buddhist concept, refers to the quality of the actions a company and its employees take as a result of that decision. All our actions should take into consideration their effect on others. We discuss Right Conduct in more detail in chapter 2.

This book is unique in applying the principles of Right View and Right Conduct to decision making in organizations. An organization is more than the sum of the individuals within it, because the organization can accomplish many things that individuals alone cannot. Yet any decision made in an organization also affects its individual members, who also have their private lives, families, friends, and memberships in other groups. As a result, each and every decision a leader in a business or organization makes has an impact on countless others.

We do not want to give the impression or claim that applying Right View and Right Conduct is easy. It is not. Reaching perfection is beyond the capability of almost everyone. What we do claim is that everyone can improve their minds and performance if they want to. And that is also true for every organization, whether small, large, private sector, public sector, charity, not for profit, or NGO.

At first glance, you might expect a large difference between business and Buddhism, but their common denominator is the importance they attach to happiness. A company that does not have happy employees, customers, and shareholders will ultimately fail. Buddha considered the main purpose of his investigations and teachings to find out why people were unhappy and what could be done to reduce suffering. His conclusion was that the root cause of suffering was self-centeredness. He referred to that conclusion as a law of nature.

Self-centeredness is also the cause of negative thoughts and actions, which can get in the way of a calm and collected mind. Cheating, lying, hiding bad intentions, aggression, anger, arrogance, jealousy, malice, and resentment all qualify as negative thoughts or emotions. When you succeed in reducing the occurrence of such negativity, you will notice that your relationships with other people quickly improve. It is simple! People would rather deal with a person who is interested in their well-being than with someone who is interested only in him- or herself. Many people are totally blind to this point, however. When they meet someone, they try to impose their ideas and convince the person of their excellence without any interest in the other person.

Once your eyes are open to the damage that can come from negative thoughts and emotions, you can recognize the value of controlling them. A useful step is to install an "early warning system," an inner voice that says, "You are getting into a state of mind that falls into the negative category. Be careful: make sure that you do not lose control of your thought processes and emotions." Most important, you want to tell yourself, "Remember, if the negative thought process is very strong, do not make any significant or irreversible decisions at this moment."

Over time, it is possible for a person to reach a stage where negative thoughts and emotions no longer emerge, or do so very seldom. It takes years of practice, of course, but the rewards are plentiful.

In the above remarks by the Dalai Lama, we see the promise of Buddhist teachings and how they might be applied in the business world. The business arena and the concepts of Buddhism seem, at first, to be an unlikely pairing. The former, primarily concerned with production, profit, and growth, seems to stand in contrast with the latter, which concerns itself with compassion for others and the well-being of humankind and our planet. Take a closer look, however, and we find that business practices and Buddhist principles are both concerned with happiness and making the right decisions. They are not such an awkward coupling after all; indeed, when working in concert they can address some of the foremost problems of our time. That, of course, is the premise of this book.

To expect rapid systematic change to the global economic system is unrealistic, and so incremental change must begin with individuals. It is the leaders of our world—in business, in government, in not-for-profit organizations—who can influence the path toward change for the rest of us. This is not to suggest that leaders are only at the "top" of an organization; leaders can be found among all ranks. But unless the leaders at the top choose the right path, the leaders lower down in the organization cannot and will not go the right way.

Right View: Developing Wisdom

As His Holiness has explained, Right View consists of two parts: the decision-making process and the three values or concepts—dependent origination, interdependence, and impermanence—that have to be respected in every decision. Leaders are faced all the time with the necessity of making decisions. When difficult decisions arise, on either a personal or a company level, the goal is to respond not from a self-centered point of view but from the point of view that takes into account the interests of the company and all the people and organizations affected by the decision. In order to achieve the best outcome, the process*—from originating the decision to taking the action and following up on its effects—must function in the best possible way, which is why the focus in decision making according to Right View is always on what the* effects *will be after implementation.*

The first point business leaders should consider in the decision-making process is the intention behind the action under consideration. First, the intention must be good, meaning that at a minimum the decision will result in no harm to others. In some cases an action is beneficial to some and unavoidably detrimental to others. Nevertheless, the utmost effort should be made, through creativity and innovation, to reduce the harm as much as possible. Throughout this book we will give many examples of the right kind of decision-making processes.

The second point is that the state of mind *of the leader and, as much as possible, that of the other people involved in the process, must be good. The challenge for the decision maker is to recognize the origination of any negative effects on the mind, such as defensiveness or anger, and to be able to return the mind to a calm, collected, and concentrated state.*

When coming to the end of the decision-making process, leaders should ask themselves: Are the effects *of this decision beneficial for my organization, and also for any others concerned? What is my motivation? Am I only seeking a benefit to myself, or did I also consider the benefits to others?*

The cause-and-effect aspect of decision making can be better understood through the Buddhist principles of dependent origination, interdependence, and impermanence, which His Holiness explains as follows:

Dependent origination (causes and conditions) is another way of stating the principle of causality: the law of cause and effect, of action and consequence. Buddhism teaches that nothing exists without a cause and nothing changes of its own accord.

There is nothing new in this principle, but being thoroughly aware of it makes a difference for the following reasons. A decision initiates change. To that change there will be innumerable reactions, some positive and some negative. Yet however competent the decision maker and however much he or she has trained his or her mind, no leader can foresee all the effects that originate from his or her actions. But leaders who have the right intention and are very thorough in thinking through the effects of their decisions will make fewer mistakes.

In this context, two other principles are important: seeing the way things really are, and looking at consequences from the

point of view of others and from many perspectives. We will return to the application of these principles throughout the book.

There is a small but interesting difference between "classic"
cause and effect and dependent origination. In dependent origination the emphasis is on the process between the cause and
the effect. When studying the process, particular attention is
paid to the conditions that made the event's occurrence possible
as well as the conditions on which the effect depended. The success of the decision always depends on many conditions, and
these have to be analyzed too.

> *I offered this business example of dependent origination
> to the Dalai Lama: Imagine a high-level executive who
> discovers that a peer in another company, one that is
> smaller and less successful, is receiving higher
> compensation than he is. His natural reaction is to judge
> this as unfair. (It would be unnatural if he were proud of
> earning a lower salary than a less successful person.) So
> he asks himself, "What should I do, if anything?" Someone
> who is unaware of the concepts of Right View and Right
> Conduct is likely to act out of self-centeredness, perhaps
> by contacting the board of directors and pointing out that
> he is underpaid and suggesting that a compensation
> consultant be engaged to analyze the situation and
> determine a fair level of compensation for him. He does
> not consider any ripple effects that his action may have on
> others, such as the cost to the organization and its other
> employees.*
>
> *On the other hand, a business leader who is aware of
> Right View and Right Conduct and who has a trained*

*mind (as discussed further in chapters 2 and 3) thinks
differently. He asks, "Is my mind influenced by greed? Am
I starting out on a path that is self-centered?" He may stop
the process immediately, or he may proceed with great
care. He may reflect on the fact that he earns far more
than is necessary to live comfortably. Of course, negative
thoughts may creep into his mind; let's say that many
businesspeople in similar positions have ski lodges in
Aspen. But he immediately recognizes this as the start of a
thought process tainted by jealousy and then asks himself,
"How would my request affect the rest of the company?"
This is a typical example of being mindful of negative
thoughts and emotions. He remembers that the company
has recently suffered layoffs. Would it be fair to ask for
more money? Would morale suffer? This kind of
questioning of the effect of his actions on others continues
until he reaches his decision.*

*In the end, the decision may be to raise the issue of
unfair compensation with his superiors, or it may not be;
but either way, the person with the trained mind has
analyzed the consequences of his action on others and is
aware that he should watch carefully for self-centered
motivation and emotions such as jealousy.*

*Of course, decisions become more complex when we
move beyond the example of the single executive to the
level of the corporation. When corporations make
decisions, even more effects have to be foreseen down the
line: financial risks; a company's reputation; the interests
of the majority of employees and all the other
stakeholders.*

Interdependence is cause and effect from a different perspective. As nothing exists without a cause, and every cause has many effects, interdependence among different phenomena is the logical consequence. Here it means focusing on our dependence on one another. All our actions and decisions have effects on ourselves and on others. My actions have an effect on other people. Their reactions to my action have an effect on me, and so on in an endless chain.

A company is a typical example of interdependence. It depends on the actions of customers, government policies, and political developments, on its employees, customers, shareholders, and distributors—actions and reactions in an endless chain.

The jewelry net of Indra provides a beautiful image of interdependence.[1] Indra is the Hindu god of the universe. He has a net in the shape of a ball. At each knot is a jewel. When one jewel emits light, that light is reflected in all the other jewels. All those reflections are then returned to the emitting jewel, and then reflected again, and so on. It may be useful for you, as a leader, to imagine yourself as one of the jewels. Each one of your actions and decisions is reflected by everyone in the net of a constantly changing, interdependent system.

Leaders realize their dependence on others but often do not fully understand how dependent they are on other people outside their control—the customers and the media, for example. But the best leaders are very aware not only of their influence on others, but also of others' influence on them and their organization.

Impermanence is another element of cause and effect that leaders must account for when making decisions. It is simple enough to say that nothing exists that is permanent and without a cause. This concept leads to a great deal of confusion, as in Buddhist literature it is referred to as "emptiness." This is an abbreviation of "empty of anything that exists inherently," that is, without a cause, totally independent. This can also be expressed differently: the only things that exist are processes operating in a network of causes and effects. People know this to be true but do not like it; they would prefer permanent, satisfactory states.

As a result, many business leaders adhere rigidly to fixed goals and objectives and hope that when reached, these will lead to a permanent satisfactory state. That is impossible. The concept of impermanence teaches us that every goal is a moving target.

Leaders and everybody else must recognize that myriad developments will occur, making it impossible to reach a steady-state goal of satisfaction without making changes. Some changes are pleasant and others not so pleasant, but we all have to face reality and make many of them. One of the greatest challenges in society today is how to cope with an increasing rate of change. Even companies that have been successful over many years will not continue to be successful forever. Laurens explains:

> *Impermanence (or "constant change") shows up everywhere in the business world. It is a familiar refrain for today's business leaders. Robert H. Rosen, founder of Healthy Companies International, puts it this way:*

>> *While travelling through Asia, I was especially struck by the Buddhist notion of impermanence. The idea is that change is the natural state of things, everything in life grows and decays, and*

uncertainty and anxiety are an inherent part of being alive. . . . I began looking beyond the office of the leaders I was meeting to see real men and women, with personal aspirations, vulnerabilities, and fears. I began to see how we all live with some degree of anxiety over much of our lives.[2]

Corporations depend on innovation, reinvention, rebranded products, and finding new ways to remain competitive in the global marketplace and satisfy changing customer requirements. For these reasons, of all the Buddhist concepts, impermanence is the one that is most readily understood by the business world. But even though they understand it, many businesses fail to accept it and often react too slowly to change, miss the next innovation wave, or introduce new products too late.

You may wonder why there is a need to have three concepts that are basically the same. It is because experience over several millennia shows that each concept activates different parts of the mind, so you gain a more thorough understanding of reality. Just try!

The Buddhist view is not fatalistic—it does not suggest that we accept change for the worse as a fact of life. On the contrary, it teaches that by being aware of constant change and trying to spot negative change at an early stage, we can avoid negative developments, and sometimes even turn them into positive opportunities. This is why businesses should continually search for positive ways to deal with change.

*Buddhism stresses that the three concepts central to
decision making—cause and effect, interdependence, and
impermanence—must move beyond intellectual
understanding. They must become "realizations"; they must
be experienced at the level of feelings and become an
integral part of the mind.*

*As long as we live in this world, we are bound to
encounter problems. If, at such times, we lose hope and
become discouraged, we diminish our ability to face
difficulties. If, on the other hand, we remember that it is
not just ourselves but everyone who has to undergo
suffering, this more realistic perspective will increase our
determination and capacity to overcome troubles. Indeed,
with this attitude, each new obstacle can be seen as yet
another valuable opportunity to improve the mind.*

*This book is designed to help business leaders develop
the ability to look at an issue from many perspectives—
short-term, long-term, from the points of view of different
stakeholders—and then to use that expanded view to make
the right decisions.*

Accepting Reality, Staying Positive

*So it is the Buddhist approach that to understand reality
fully—to see and accept things the way they really are—
a person must accept Right View and have considerable
control over negative emotions such as anger or jealousy.
Two phenomena that are often obstacles to seeing reality*

are wishful thinking and thinking about problems of the past as if they still exist today.

Wishful thinking is quite common in business. The marketplace requires businesspeople to make progress, to have confidence in their direction. A businessperson with a pessimistic nature is unlikely to succeed. However, the desire to be successful leads many businesspeople to reject negative information. A clear example of this is when employees experience a problem in the workplace and wait a long time to bring it to the attention of their manager. They may be hoping that the problem will go away on its own so they do not have to be a messenger of bad news. When they see a colleague getting involved in something very negative, like corruption, they are reluctant to report it, as they fear, rightly so in many cases, that they will be punished. Situations like these arise quite often and illustrate why top management is so often unaware of problems until they have become very serious and thus even more difficult to correct. Consider this maxim employed by one company: "Good news must travel slowly. Bad news should travel quickly."[3] Adopting this frame of mind helps companies remain better informed of potential problems before they become liabilities. Avoiding wishful thinking is an effective way to become aware of reality before it is too late.

Thinking about problems of the past as if they are reality today is another way to express this concept of transferring experiences of the past into the present. If a negative thought process is allowed to take hold, a great deal of energy is wasted on being upset and angry about a past event. Many businesspeople fall into the trap of spending a great deal of emotional energy being upset about injustices that they or their companies have suffered in the past. Dwelling on the past as if it were the present is not only a distortion of reality, it is a waste of time.

Take the story of Thitinart na Patalung, chief executive of Working Diamond in Thailand. Thitinart was very successful in business until she lost everything when her business partner cheated her. As a result, she became very depressed and angry. At the suggestion of a friend, however, she decided to attend a meditation course. When she started her meditation, one of the first things that entered her mind was the face of this disloyal partner, and she became furious on the spot. After calming herself down, she was able to analyze her thought process. She started to realize that by conjuring up the betrayal in her mind over and over again, she was experiencing as "real" something that was only in her head. She compared the development of this intense anger about past events to someone holding a piece of broken glass in his hand and squeezing the glass until his hand bleeds, then squeezing some more and producing more blood. She found that realizing that the anger she experienced existed only in her mind enabled her to see reality and get rid of her bitterness about the past.

Decisions are made primarily to change something. Change is often thought of as moving from one static situation to another, but this is a dangerous simplification. The present situation is the result of innumerable causes and conditions; it is also dependent on many causes and conditions, and it is changing all the time. Recognizing this interdependence and impermanence helps us understand the complexity of change and make successful decisions. It also leads to a holistic, rather than narrowminded, view of change. In other words, before a decision is made, leaders should take the Right View and consider the consequences from many different perspectives. Acceptance of impermanence should also strengthen your resolve to monitor how decisions are executed.

Right View is a fairly easy concept to understand, but applying it properly requires skill. Every situation is unique, and there are no automatic answers. Having a grasp of the principles is the first step, but the decision maker still has to think a great deal, learn how to cope with conflicting objectives, weigh short- and long-term consequences, and consider different interests. This is what we mean when we talk about Right Conduct. Right Conduct requires practice, and only with practice comes skill.

Developing the Right View is the foundation on which the remainder of the concepts in this book are based. It is impossible to achieve positive change with the wrong view.

The following chapters explain how to combine Right View with Right Conduct and how to find a disciplined practice that works for you and your particular circumstances. Keep Right View and Right Conduct always active in your mind, and good decision making will then follow.

2

Doing the Right Thing

In Buddhism we consider it very important that people teaching Buddhist principles apply those principles in their own conduct. In India at the time of Buddha, teachers and philosophers were taken seriously only if they lived as they preached. This is not as easy as it sounds; moving from theory to practice when it comes to human behavior requires determination and effort. But it is an important target for leaders to strive for.

The same principle applies to true leaders as to these early philosophers. A leader will be respected only when he acts according to the principles in which he says he believes. Many people imitate the behavior of their leaders. If that behavior is different from the stated principles, people will follow the behavior and not the principles.

In Buddhism, a person is considered to be the accumulation of all his actions up to that point in time. Good actions make a person good, bad actions bad. The effect of bad actions can be reduced by subsequent good actions. This is referred to as the law of karma. And karma is just as important for people who lead in businesses and organizations as it is for spiritual or religious leaders.

In chapter 1 we saw that the quality of decision making depends on using the principles of Right View and on the skill and energy with which these principles are applied. Through determination and practice (also known as training the mind), anyone can achieve a greater ability to choose the right path. This is particularly effective for leaders, as they make decisions that impact their organizations and the people who work for them. These decisions take the form of policies and practices as well as the functional roles that individuals play. In plain terms, managers must serve the needs of the whole organization as well as those of individual workers. This is Right Conduct.

It often seems that leaders are put in a no-win situation, as these needs can be at odds with one another. The Dalai Lama's answer to that conundrum would be this. The principle is simple: the effect of the decision should be beneficial to the organization and to any others affected. Harm is to be avoided. In reality, a decision may produce benefits for some but disadvantages for others. In such a case, choose the way that benefits the largest number of people.

The situation is even more difficult when it is impossible to avoid harming some people. The Buddhist principle is that if harm cannot be avoided, it must eliminate a much greater harm to other people. There is a three-stage decision-making process. Make your initial decision and check whether the result is any harm to anyone. If not, you can go ahead. If so, apply your creativity to find another solution that eliminates the harm. If it is completely impossible to avoid harm of some sort, then you have to make certain that this harm is justified because it avoids a much greater harm or because it leads to huge benefits for some other people. For example, if a company is in a financial crisis because its sales have fallen dramatically, it can justify laying people off, because while those people will be harmed, the jobs of a far greater number of remaining employees will be saved. Of course, it would have been better if the crisis had been avoided in the first place, but crises do happen.

A good leader must develop the capability to deal with such situations so that people both inside and outside the organization consider the decisions made to be fair ones. It is not enough that the decision is fair, though: the leader must also communicate the rationale for the decision in an effective way to the people concerned.

Making decisions and taking action are critical parts of leadership. However, not just any action will do. Often managers make decisions for the sake of "ticking a box," but this is a faulty tactic. This chapter describes how the actions taken must be wholesome ones, meaning that they are ethical in nature and arise from an awareness of Right View and a trained mind. Out of these ethical decisions, advises the Buddha, comes peace. Not taking action can be an unwholesome act in itself, in that sometimes standing by can bring about suffering. So how does one learn when, and how, to take the right action?

Taking Ethical Actions

*After Kenneth Lay, former chief executive of Enron, was
convicted in 2006 of fraud and conspiracy charges, one of
his collaborators made the following remark: "We want
honest leaders who are decisive, creative, optimistic and
even courageous. But often we don't even look for one of
the most critical traits of a leader: humility."[1] A humble
leader listens to others. He or she values input from
employees, even if it is bad news, and humility is marked
by an ability to admit mistakes.*

*Most people would say that some measure of humility is
an essential trait of a leader. But there are other
characteristics as well—kindness, a sense of equanimity,
even self-confidence—that are considered to be important
in Buddhism. These are best described as "wholesome" (as
opposed to "unwholesome") actions and attitudes, and
there is a recommended process for "throwing out"
(ejecting) the bad ones and "welcoming in" (replacing them
with) the good.*

In Buddhism we have the concept of wholesome and unwholesome tendencies, both in thought and in action. Wholesome
tendencies—such as self-confidence, heedfulness, and concentration—lead to physical and moral well-being and ethical
actions; unwholesome tendencies—such as distraction, careless-
ness, thoughtlessness, and forgetfulness—result in suffering and
harm and can, therefore, be seen as unethical. People can have
both wholesome and unwholesome tendencies; the task is
therefore to remove the unwholesome tendencies and fill the

vacated space with wholesome ones. An important point is that wholesome and unwholesome actions and thoughts are mutually exclusive: a person cannot be angry and calm at the same time or concentrated and distracted at the same time.

For our purposes here, we are focusing on the contrast between wholesome and unwholesome mental factors.[2] (Throughout the book, we will also refer to these factors as "positive" and "negative" emotions.) If we combine the wholesome and unwholesome factors in mutually exclusive pairs (e.g., calmness and anger), it becomes easy to see which we should get rid of—eject—and which one to put in its place. We give a couple of examples here; you can find the remaining pairs at the end of the chapter.

So how can a leader eject unwholesome tendencies? The first step is to think about the emotion and draw conclusions as to whether it is making a constructive contribution (this is called analytical meditation and will be discussed in more detail in chapter 3). The second step is to apply one-pointed meditation (also discussed in chapter 3) to that conclusion in order to replace the emotion with a positive one.

Although these concepts may seem removed from the business world, in fact that is not the case. If leaders in business could replace unhealthy mental attitudes with healthy ones, better leadership would follow at once. The age-old phrase "lead by example" is at work here. A leader with a trained mind becomes the one to emulate.

Self-Confidence vs. Insecurity

According to Buddha, the greatest treasure humans can have is self-confidence. Leaders and heads of companies often appear self-confident, but for many this is a facade. Leaders often suffer from lack of confidence because they are not sure that what they are doing is right. In my view, lack of self-confidence is a waste of time because it does not contribute to finding the right solutions. To combat this, leaders must apply the concept of dependent origination in everyday life (see chapter 1). By that I mean that they must make wise decisions by taking all factors into account. Once those in charge start thinking in this interconnected way, they feel the rightness of their actions — and self-confidence builds from there.

Heedfulness and Concentration vs. Distraction, Carelessness, Thoughtlessness, and Forgetfulness

Heedfulness means, quite simply, paying close attention. People are quite perceptive in their ability to judge this quality. If you are not listening to someone when you are in conversation with him or her, chances are he or she will know and effective communication will become all but impossible. Giving your full concentration and attention to the other person is considered not only good manners but also ethical or wholesome.

> *Heedfulness is particularly important in a business leader. If a leader truly listens, it makes those he or she leads feel valued and important, and in turn inspires them to lead.*
>
> *Take the Dalai Lama, for example. I have met hundreds of busy people over the years, and few, if any, have as large a workload as he does. But when I speak with him, I feel that he has 100 percent concentration on what I am saying. We've never been interrupted by a phone call or visitor,*

and yet I know that his time is very valuable. If a leader can convey a similar sense that all the people in his or her care are that important to him or her, trust is the result. And out of trust come all kinds of possibilities.

The process of learning how to eject the unwanted action and replace it with the desired one is useful for any individual. It will seem an obvious point that if unwholesome factors and emotions are ejected and replaced by wholesome factors, more time can be spent on productive mental activity, and there will be less suffering and more well-being as a result. There can be more "getting on with it" and less "cleaning up" after poor decisions have been made. To implement the process requires developing a certain skill set: the power of observation, the practice of discipline, and a fair dose of patience as well.

Valuing Right Livelihood

One of the main decisions we make in life is how to earn a living. The Buddhist concept of Right Livelihood means that one should earn one's living in a righteous way and that wealth should be gained in a righteous way, legally and peacefully. The Buddha mentions four specific activities that harm other beings and that one should avoid for this reason: dealing in weapons; dealing in living beings (including raising animals for slaughter, as well as the slave trade and prostitution); working in meat production and butchery; and selling intoxicants and poisons, such as alcohol and drugs. However, there are times when these activities are justified, as they are necessary to alleviate a greater degree of human suffering. Furthermore, any other occupation that would violate the principles of Right Conduct should be avoided.

The definition of Right Livelihood as "acting in a righteous way, legally and peacefully" presents the main principles. The four specific activities deserve some comment.

I strongly believe that war is wrong, but that it was justified when the Allies liberated Europe and Asia from German and Japanese occupation. Then, arms were essential. In all other circumstances, everything possible should be done to avoid the necessity of using arms.

While dealing in human beings is, of course, considered wrong everywhere in the world, raising animals for slaughter and meat production is commonplace in all countries. Most but not all Buddhist monks are vegetarians. I was raised as a vegetarian, but after a serious illness doctors told me I had to eat some meat, which I have done since.

Selling illegal drugs is obviously wrong; yet selling intoxicants such as alcohol is common in all countries, and therefore it is an individual's right.

Given these caveats, someone who acts with the right intentions, Right View, and Right Conduct is likely to earn his or her living in the right way.

The Six Perfections

The Six Perfections—often expressed as generosity, ethical discipline, patience, enthusiastic effort, concentration, and wisdom—are of obvious value to all individuals, not just leaders who want to take the Right Conduct. But a leader who possesses these traits has a distinct ability to affect others in profound ways.

Generosity

The cause of many business scandals is the greed of those in power. Greed for money and prestige is quite the opposite of generosity. Even though good performance by the chief executive is essential for the success of the company, the actual results are achieved through the collaboration of everyone within the organization. A leader who wants to take all the credit destroys other people's motivation. A good chief executive must be very generous in giving credit where it is due. Most leaders of successful organizations are in fact modest people who attribute good results to their team and who generously reward their employees for a job well done.

Generosity should be combined with wisdom. To be generous in solving only a short-term problem is not acceptable. Generosity must consider short- and long-term effects.

Ethical Discipline

When I think of ethical discipline, I am reminded of the advice given to other rulers by a king who was notably successful in governing his realm: "The best way for a ruler to reign over his country is first of all to rule himself." By "ruling himself" the king meant withstanding temptation—in other words, ethical discipline. Most kings want to be rich, admired, respected, and successful. Unless the actions used to reach such objectives are governed by moral restraint, the result will be trouble in the kingdom. Likewise, leaders in an organization who don't lead with ethical discipline put their companies, their employees, and their shareholders at risk. One needs only to recall the fate of Enron to see that this is the case. It is not wrong to become wealthy if the wealth is earned honestly and without harming others or the environment, but it is not acceptable for a person or people at the head of a company to become very wealthy while the company itself collapses, shareholders lose their savings, and employees lose their jobs.

This is not to say that ethical discipline is easy to achieve. I often refer to it as "taming the mind." An undisciplined mind is like an elephant. If left to blunder around out of control, it will wreak havoc. The main problem is to get control of our negative motivations and emotions, such as greed, self-centeredness, anger, hatred, lust, fear, lack of self-confidence, and jealousy. We can conceive of the nature of the mind in terms of water in a lake. When the water is stirred up (by negative thoughts or emotions), mud from the lake's bottom clouds it. When the storm has passed, the mud settles and the water (the mind) is left clear again. The "storm" refers to the effect of negative motivations and emotions. Prior to every action, we should rid ourselves of all negative thoughts, so that we are "free" to respond. Until we have learned to discipline our minds to rid ourselves of all negative thoughts, we will have difficulty seeing reality clearly, and in turn will be unable to make the right decisions.

Patience

Patience must be cultivated. It is the only way to be prepared when provocative circumstances occur, such as hostility, criticism, or disappointment. In the case of anger, it is not the ability to suppress it but the ability to remain calm in the face of it that counts. To do so requires great patience, which is achieved only by training the mind.

Of course, patience should be understood as "justified patience"; in some cases, immediate action is necessary. But in most cases, taking the time to gather one's thoughts before responding to negative situations will yield the most positive results. Deciding whether or not to exercise patience requires good judgment.

Enthusiastic Effort

Our level of enthusiasm depends on our belief in the importance of the goals we want to reach and our motivation to get there. I've heard it said that "enthusiasm is contagious," meaning that people have enormous reserves of energy that can be mobilized with enthusiasm. Being able to encourage this enthusiasm for things that matter is an essential trait in a leader.

Concentration

By "concentration" I refer to the ability to focus all your mental energy on one issue. Most people have very poor concentration, bouncing from one thing to the next. They waste a lot of time thinking about things that went wrong in the past (which, as I mentioned in chapter 1, is a grave obstacle to seeing reality) or worrying about the future. Leaders are not immune to this. However, people who cannot concentrate are unable to focus their minds, which is essential for improving the quality of their decisions.

Wisdom

Wisdom is essentially possessing Right View—the ability to see things as they are. In the business world, wise leaders are those who use Right View and Right Conduct to decide what has to be done today to safeguard the long-term future of the company or organization.

Reaping the Benefits

I have interviewed many executives in Asia who are very enthusiastic about the benefits they have gained from applying the principles of Right View and Right Conduct and from training the mind through meditation, as we outline in chapter 3.

For instance, a decade ago Thai business leaders were facing an economic crisis. Several came close to declaring bankruptcy. But those who were practicing Buddhists noted that compared to colleagues in other companies, they had been able to respond to this adversity with a greater sense of calm and with clearer deliberation. What's more, when asked about their views of the purpose of business, none answered that the primary goals involved profit or shareholder value. One manager, who was responsible for a very profitable company, commented, "The main weakness of managers in the West is that they are too concerned about the bottom line. In all my business dealings, I make sure that my customers get a good deal . . . but also our company. Profit comes as a result."

These managers were able to characterize their skills as follows:

- *Increased ability to deal with a crisis. One manager said that almost all the other managers in his sector had gone to the banks to ask for some forgiveness of debt. He was one of the few who had not tried. He admitted to having been very worried, but opted instead to talk with his Buddhist teacher. The teacher told him, "I understand nothing of your problems, but if you calm down and meditate, I am sure you will find a solution." At first this may have been seen as dismissive, but the manager followed his advice successfully.*

- *Better decision making. The managers said that they agonized less about making the wrong decisions and felt that they had a better frame of reference within which to make decisions. They found it easier to concentrate on the issues and had become more self-confident in their choices.*

- *Better relations with the people directly reporting to them. The Buddhist leaders ascribed their good relations to having more patience when dealing with controversy or employee-relations issues. They described a willingness to look at an issue several times and did not feel threatened by appearing indecisive at first.*

- *Fewer meetings and better execution of decisions. Several of the CEOs reported that fewer meetings were required because they had learned to concentrate and give their undivided attention to the item at hand. They listened more carefully to colleagues when decisions were being made and when the execution of those decisions was discussed.*

- *More creativity. The head of an architectural firm in Taiwan named Kris Yao described his increased creativity as a result of his mind training: "Before I started mind training, like most architects, I was very keen on designing something unique, different from what others were doing. I hoped that people seeing my buildings would admire their unique beauty and that I might become one of the famous architects." Yao had accompanied the Dalai Lama on one of his visits to Taiwan and had become inspired by Buddhist ideas. He said, "I have let go of that ambition and instead concentrate on what is best for the client and the people that will 'live in' the building. I found that my creativity increased. My clients are more satisfied than before, and I am more satisfied too."*

- *A high level of enthusiasm for their jobs. All these leaders were enthusiastic about their jobs and about the benefits they felt they had experienced from being active Buddhists and training their minds. This enthusiasm pervaded their work.*

The managers in the above examples understood and practiced Right Conduct and Right View, no doubt because they have systematically begun to change their thought processes and resulting behaviors. If you examine these examples closely, the benefits that result from these leaders' actions are all due to a reduction in unwholesome mental tendencies. Their view that "Buddhism has no impact on action unless you practice" is very telling. What they are getting at is that change is cultivated over time, once you begin to replace poorer actions with better ones. It is encouraging to know that Buddhism has a great deal of knowledge to bring to the modern corporation—and to the global economy.

To make real progress, not only do you have to change the way you act as an individual; the organization in which you work has to change as well. This too can be done successfully by applying the principles of Right View and Right Conduct. Remember, Right View means that you will at all times be actively concerned not only for your own well-being but also for that of others. Right Conduct means that you accept the hard work necessary to apply the principles of Right View. True leaders will bring these disciplined practices into their places of work. That is what the next section of this book is about.

Welcoming in the Good

Here are the remaining pairs of wholesome and unwholesome mental factors. Through meditation, you can throw out the bad and welcome in the good.

HUMILITY EJECTS UNJUSTIFIED PRIDE, INFLATED SELF-ESTEEM, CONCEIT, AND ARROGANCE

Humility may appear to be the opposite of self-confidence. However, for people who experience continued success, self-confidence can escalate into unjustified (or false) pride. When leaders start to think that all their successes are due to their own brilliance and decisiveness, they have lost a sense of humility and instead have inflated self-esteem. They forget that their success depends on many other people—and probably on some luck as well. The important point here is to remember that no success is solely yours and to remain humble in the face of it. People can recognize humility instantly in a leader and find it an inspiring trait.

CONSIDERATION AND ACTIVE CONCERN
FOR THE WELL-BEING OF OTHERS
EJECT NOT CONSIDERING POSSIBLE HARM TO OTHERS

Being concerned for the well-being of others is central to the overall concept of Right Conduct: every action we take should consider its effect on others. Consideration for others is on this list because it is one of the wholesome factors; however, beyond being a positive characteristic of leaders, consideration should also become a state of mind. Anyone, but particularly a leader in society, should come to consider the well-being of others first and foremost, no matter what decision he or she is facing.

EQUANIMITY . . .

"Equanimity" essentially means calmness of mind and is a very important mental factor. It is in fact better described as evenness of emotion; one who has equanimity is seen as open-minded, peaceful, and without bias. Equanimity is often referred to as the absence of self-centered desire or craving. Although this may not conjure up a dynamic driver of a business, it portrays a person you can trust—arguably the most essential quality of leadership.

. . . EJECTS CRAVING FOR POWER, WEALTH, AND FAME

There is nothing wrong with desiring wealth if it is honestly earned, or with desiring fame if that fame is for making a positive contribution. Desire is a word that can be easily misconstrued. For example, desire can be positive if it is used for achieving a wholesome state of mind, but negative when it refers to desiring undeserved wealth. When referring to the negative type of desire, we therefore use the word "craving," which refers to an insatiable desire for wealth or fame. As there are always more famous and wealthier people, a person with such a craving will never be happy. Even worse is that people with such cravings are likely to take shortcuts to achieve their aims, including harming others and breaking laws. People who do not control their cravings become slaves to this unwholesome emotion.

. . . EJECTS DEJECTION OR WORRY WHEN FAILING TO REACH OBJECTIVES OR EXPERIENCING DISAPPOINTMENTS

It is natural for a manager to be worried when something goes wrong, such as if one of his or her best collaborators leaves or if it is discovered that the company has been involved in something unethical (such as price fixing) without his or her knowledge, or if the company has to report a loss instead of a profit. Worry is a waste of energy, however. It does not solve anything. To get rid of worry is not easy. But meditating on the uselessness of it and dropping the emotion as soon as it manifests itself (without violently suppressing it) eventually will lead to equanimity.

. . . EJECTS HATRED, ANGER, WRATH, RESENTMENT, SPITE, ENVY, AND JEALOUSY

Anger, hatred, and resentment can be very strong emotions. But they are unproductive, waste energy, can cause suffering, and may lead to distraction. The method for ejecting these time-wasting energies is much the same as for worry. By meditating on the uselessness of these emotions, you can move beyond them into the desired state of equanimity, or composure and calmness of mind.

A SENSE OF SHAME EJECTS SHAMELESSNESS

Shame may look like a strange factor on this list, as it is often thought of as a negative emotion. People sometimes make mistakes; that is unavoidable. I consider shame to be positive, however, when it leads to corrective action. And the absence of shame is dangerous, as it means that a person lacks minimal moral standards. In this context, though, guilt is less useful than shame. Guilt appears to be something permanent, about which nothing can be done. From that point of view, it is unwholesome. It is better to turn guilt into shame, which in turn leads to remedial action. Buddhists believe that bad actions will have inevitable negative consequences on the person who committed the action. The only way to reduce these negative consequences is to counter them with good actions. Shame is often the motivation for doing so.

KINDNESS EJECTS INDIFFERENCE, HOSTILITY, IRRITABILITY, ILL HUMOR, AND DISLIKE

When I meet someone, I always think of that person as a fellow human being, someone who wants to be happy, like me. If the person acts in a hostile or unfriendly manner, I try to differentiate between the way they are acting and the person himself. Buddhists believe that within every person is a wholesome or pure core, and that by extending kindness and friendship, hostility is diminished. Nothing can be gained by being unfriendly, though it is not necessary to withhold comment if a person is acting wrongly or holds wrong views. When confronted with negative emotions such as hostility and indifference, leaders should attempt to replace these emotions with kindness. In an organization where a leader is kind to his employees, they will in turn be kinder to one another and to their customers.

VIGOR REPLACES DULLNESS OF MIND OR SLOTH

Striving for vigor is not likely to be a problem for leaders, as a high energy level is necessary to cope with the demands of their heavy workload. Without vigor, an executive cannot succeed. However, for a company to succeed, this energy must spread throughout the ranks. Leaders should find the best ways to promote it, whether simply by example or through explicit policies. The more vigor employees have, the more productive they will be.

FLEXIBILITY AND AN OPEN MIND EJECT FANATICISM
AND BLIND FAITH

Having an open mind is very important for today's leaders. More and more, flexibility is needed in the business world, as business decisions become more complex and their effects become more global and farther reaching. There are few absolute truths in business today. A leader should be careful about becoming fanatical and avoid putting blind faith in his or her decisions. Leaders in companies need to keep an open mind about the rightness of their decisions and be flexible enough to change directions when necessary.

3

Training Your Mind

Applying the principles of Right View and Right Conduct is a major challenge. Only a very gifted leader will be able to do so perfectly without training his or her mind.

I have trained my mind since I was very young. I still continue to do so, every day for several hours, both when I travel and when I am at home. My experience is that, with time, training the mind becomes a habit, like eating meals.

The good news is that you can make progress with a very modest investment of time. Reaching perfection is beyond the capabilities of almost everyone; therefore, the main point is to aim for steady progress.

The challenges a leader faces and the number of potentially difficult decisions that have to be made within a limited amount of time can be daunting. The purpose of training the mind is to be able to be calm, collected, and concentrated in all circumstances. This will enable the mind to analyze decisions quickly and from many perspectives. That requires an open and supple mind; a closed and rigid mind will not do.

The untrained mind can be compared to a monkey swinging from branch to branch, wandering from one subject to another, without concentration. When the mind is disturbed by anger, jealousy, hate, impatience, fear, lack of self-confidence, or negative emotions about things that happened in the past, it is wasting valuable time that instead should be used for constructive thinking. The purpose of training the mind is to maximize its power by focusing it on the decisions that matter. Laurens writes:

> For those more familiar with Western psychology than Eastern philosophy, the process of training the mind is also sometimes referred to as "conditioning," meaning training your behavior to be independent of any event in the environment. For example, if you tend to get angry and defensive as soon as you are criticized, you can condition yourself to instead listen attentively and analyze whether there is something to learn from the situation. Your actions depend on the conclusion you reach. The automatic reaction of becoming defensive when criticized is therefore replaced by the automatic reaction of listening with an open mind. To put it another way, conditioning your mind has changed your automatic reaction to criticism.
>
> Over hundreds of years, Buddhists have developed many exercises to train the mind. In the second part of this chapter we will present seven of these exercises, in order of increasing complexity, that ordinary people who are neither specialists nor Buddhists can practice. But first, I

want to answer several questions that are frequently asked
about training the mind.

How Can You Find Time to Meditate?

Anyone, even a busy executive, can find five minutes a day
for the mental exercises outlined in this chapter. There are
many ways to find time to practice. The delays of business
life—waiting in an airport or a taxi, for example—
provide opportunities to incorporate your practice into
your daily life. Instead of being irritated when these
delays occur, count these occasions as excellent
opportunities for training the mind.

I used to be very uncomfortable whenever I had to wait.
If I arrived at the airport and saw that there were long
queues, it immediately made me nervous. Once in a queue,
I would worry that I should have chosen another, faster-
moving line. I finally concluded that my behavior was silly
and adopted another way of looking at it. Now when I see
a long queue, I think of it as a perfect opportunity for
training my mind.

Remember that short stretches of five minutes, although
not optimal times for meditation, do still have value. Many
Buddhist executives have found ways to incorporate
meditation into their daily routines at work. It need not be
viewed as disruptive to the flow of activity, but rather as
a welcome interlude when moments of calm or clarity are
called for.

Should You Train on Your Own
or with a Teacher?

Choosing a qualified spiritual teacher is an important decision in one's spiritual life.[1] Before accepting someone as your spiritual teacher, you must examine that person thoroughly. In Tibet we say, "Don't act like a dog finding a lump of meat." In other words, you should not choose someone just because they may have an important title or widespread influence. A teacher is your guide on the spiritual path, and therefore he (or she) should practice what he teaches. Real guidance can come only from the teacher's own experience, not on the basis of mere intellectual understanding. The teacher should at least be gentle and have tamed his own mind, because the very purpose of adopting someone as your spiritual master is to tame your mind. The teacher should be someone who can answer your questions directly and help you to clarify your doubts.

Once you have accepted someone as your teacher, it is essential to cultivate a proper sense of faith in him and respect and abide by his instructions. But faith and respect do not imply blind faith. The Buddha, the greatest of teachers, explained that a pupil should heed the teacher's virtuous instructions but disregard "unwholesome" commands. He pointed out the importance of being skeptical about what teachers teach. He wrote:

> Just as people test the purity of gold by burning it in
> fire, by cutting it and examining it on a touchstone, so
> exactly you should do, accept my words after subjecting
> them to a critical test and not out of reverence for me.[2]

There are two ways to approach Buddhist teachings, the intelligent way and the unintelligent way. The intelligent way is to approach the scriptures and their commentaries with skepticism and an open mind and to try to relate them to your own experience and understanding. Such a student will not follow a teaching or a scripture simply because it is attributed to a famous master. Rather, he or she will judge the validity of the content on the basis of that student's own understanding, derived through personal investigation and analysis. The intelligent way can be expressed as follows: "Rely on the message of the teacher, not on the person of the teacher. Rely on the meaning, not just on the words." However, it is also possible to train one's mind without a spiritual teacher. As Laurens writes:

> *You can practice the walking, breathing, and mantra-citing techniques described at the end of this chapter without a teacher. When I attended a retreat in Thailand, I found that learning in a group makes it easier. That is surprising, in a way, because you do not talk for a whole week to any of the participants. But sitting on the floor in the same room with many others, all trying to meditate, gave me extra force. Spending an entire week talking for only fifteen minutes a day to monks also had a positive effect on my concentration.*
>
> *Learning these techniques of meditation does require patience. Making some progress is relatively easy, but becoming really proficient takes many years.*

What Is the Effect of Meditation on My Brain and Health?

Recent studies have produced some very interesting facts regarding how the brain changes as the result of meditation.[3] Until the 1990s, it was believed that the number of neurons in the brain was constant throughout one's life. It has now been proved that the brain generates new neurons when an action is repeated a great deal (for example, among concert pianists the part of the brain that gives instructions to the fingers becomes enlarged) or if a person learns something new. Today, through new technologies, such as the electroencephalogram (EEG), that "map" the brain's activity, we can understand far more about how the brain responds to repeated action like meditation.

The first brain experiment regarding meditation was carried out on a Tibetan monk who had done meditation exercises for more than thirty years. The researchers compared the brain maps of 175 people who had never meditated to the brain map of the monk. They found that the monk's activity in the frontal lobe, which is associated with greater happiness, was higher than that of any of the 175 other people tested. That was promising evidence for the positive effects of meditation! The question arose, however, whether this monk might have been a unique case.

The next experiment was carried out with employees of a biotech laboratory. All these volunteers traveled to the University of Massachusetts, where their brains were measured with an EEG. Next, the group was split in two;

*half were put through a ten-week meditation program,
and half were not. Those in the meditation program
attended a two- to three-hour session held by a
professional meditation teacher every week. They were
also asked to meditate for forty-five minutes a day between
the sessions. At the end of the ten-week program, a one-
day retreat was held. The EEG was again performed on
those who had participated in the meditation and those
who had not. The meditation group showed a significant
increase in activity in the left frontal lobe since the start of
the meditation and more activity than those who hadn't
had the meditation training. The participants also
reported that their anxiety level and their negative
emotions decreased after the meditation training.*

*The meditation was even shown to have had a positive
impact on the immune systems of those who had received
the training. When the subjects in both groups were given
an influenza vaccine after the meditation program had
ended, blood samples showed that the meditation group
had a stronger immune response to the vaccine. This was
not a total surprise, as it was already known that high
activity in the left frontal lobe predicts that a person's
immune system will respond better to a vaccine.*

*Further research at Harvard has found similar
startling results about the health benefits of meditation.*

*An instructor at Harvard Medical School scanned the
brains of twenty people with a long history of meditating
for forty minutes a day. When she compared their brain
images to those of nonmeditating people of similar ages
and backgrounds, she found that the meditators had 5*

percent thicker brain tissue in the prefrontal cortex.[4] *In
other words, meditation had seemingly enlarged the part
of the brain that regulates emotion, attention, and
working memory.*

How Can You Start Learning to Meditate?

When you read about all the meditation exercises I'm about to
list, you may become disheartened or overwhelmed, as you cannot possibly learn all of them at once. My recommendation is
to start with the simplest exercises and spend just a few minutes
a day on them. If you like the experience, gradually increase
the time you spend on them and add exercises little by little.
When you arrive at a point when you want to make more rapid
progress, consider spending a week in a retreat, as Laurens did.

> *When I decided I wanted to learn to meditate, I attended a
> ten-day meditation retreat in Thailand. After three days of
> lectures, a one-week retreat started, during which the only
> activities were walking and sitting. As a contrast to my
> daily life, I found it extraordinary not to talk to or even
> make eye contact with any of the participants for an entire
> week. I quickly learned, however, that it is this lack of
> external distraction that produces a kind of serene focus. I
> was taught to rotate the walking and sitting meditations
> throughout any given day. Since that time, I have added
> the other meditation techniques and I practice almost
> every day. People tell me I have since become calmer and
> more pleasant to deal with.*

Here are some simple techniques to help get you started on the rewarding path of meditation.

Simple Techniques for Busy Leaders

1. *Walking meditation*

Walking meditation may be the simplest form of meditation to try, particularly for fast-moving Westerners. Its purpose is to develop mindfulness and concentration. "Mindfulness" refers to the ability to observe when emotions and thoughts become active in the brain. For example, when you are criticized you might notice that instead of listening intently, you start thinking, "This is unpleasant. I must defend myself. I do not like this person." In addition to noticing when a negative thought or emotion starts, mindfulness involves the capability to "drop" the emotion or stop the thought. This must be done peacefully, not by trying to suppress it. The instruction is "note and drop."

When we perform walking meditation, we are using the physical acts of our bodies to bring us into greater awareness. It is the act of moving one foot in front of the other that brings us into focus and helps clear our minds.

The correct way to practice walking meditation is to walk evenly and naturally. Walk with your body *and* your mind. In other words, when your body is walking, let your mind be aware of the walking too, rather than allowing your mind to follow the ordinary path, which is to dwell on a problem or think about the past or the future. If you feel your mind start to wander, bring it back to the physical act of walking, to feeling the rhythmic nature of your steps. Let there be mindfulness, clear awareness of and complete attentiveness to your walking body. Here are some key ways to do this:

- Note your body. Walk very slowly and focus your attention on your feet, noting the movement and placement of each step. Train your mind to be aware of the steps—left foot, right foot, and so on—and continually remind yourself to keep your attention there.

- Note your mind. Be aware of the activity of your mind as you walk. When an emotion or a thought emerges, note whether it is pleasant, unpleasant, or neutral, but do not attach any sentiment to that thought. Then let it go by bringing your attention back to your physical movements.

Walking meditation is an excellent way of developing our awareness in our ordinary lives. Many people consider it the easiest method of cultivating mindfulness because it can be incorporated into everyday life without much disruption. I urge everyone to try this method of meditation first, mostly because it does not require much behavioral change; you can practice it incrementally throughout the day as you go about your business.

2. Sitting meditation

The purpose of sitting meditation is the same as that of walking meditation, except that the concentration is on the breath instead of on the movement of the feet. When practicing sitting meditation, we are more inclined to turn off external distractions and to focus on the process of meditating. Here is how:

Sit cross-legged on the floor, or instead on a firm chair. What is important is to make sure that your back is straight and that you are not leaning on anything (which would give rise to excessive comfort and lead to sleepiness). It does not matter which posture you use; what is important is that your sitting position is comfortable and stable. A straight, unsupported back allows you to sit comfortably for a long period without putting great effort into balancing yourself. This is to prevent you from worrying about your body, because the development of the mind through calm and insightful meditation is a subtle process.

Breathe in deeply, then breathe out with a slow and long breath. Breathe in deeply again, fully, stretch your body, and again breathe out with a slow and long breath. Repeat twenty-four times. Be aware of your sitting body; be aware of the exhalation and the inhalation. If your mind wanders to other thoughts, then as soon as you are aware of the thought, drop it and return to being mindful of your breath.

Sitting meditation requires a bit more time and preparation than walking meditation, but for that reason it can also yield more profound results. As Laurens recalls:

> *My experience with this exercise in the beginning was that*
> *it was more difficult than walking meditation. I found it*
> *easier to concentrate on the movement of the feet than on*
> *the breath, which is a required component of sitting*
> *meditation. The objective is the same as with walking*
> *meditation — to gain control over the emergence of*
> *thoughts and emotions — but the passivity and stillness*

required of sitting meditation (not to mention the cross-legged position!) are more physically challenging.

Both walking and sitting meditation will help you gain better control over negative emotions, reduce the amount your mind wanders, and improve concentration. But these results won't come immediately, or even after the first few sessions. As with all forms of meditation, consistent practice is the key.

Here are some other techniques you can try while practicing sitting meditation:

A WESTERN BREATHING TECHNIQUE

Many people know that if you get worried or stressed, taking deep breaths can be an effective way of calming down. The simple act of breathing is also an effective meditation technique. Like walking meditation, focusing on the physical act of breathing can improve concentration and clear the mind.

We think of breathing as an effortless act and thus often don't give it much thought. But the way we breathe tells all; it is a reflection of our emotions and our ability to handle stress. Do you hold your breath when under pressure? Do you start breathing faster when you need to make a decision quickly and the stakes are high? What happens to your breathing as you experience the ups and downs of life?

Many people are not aware of their breathing patterns. In Buddhism, we consider breathing to be our connection with a vital life force. If we use it properly, its natural rhythm can lead to a feeling of calm. The next time you find yourself in a trying situation, take note of how you are breathing. Notice the tempo and rhythm of each breath. If your breath seems strained, control it so that it falls into a slow, natural rhythm once again. As you breathe in, fill up your belly and lungs, and as you exhale, press out the air so that your belly contracts. Surprisingly, many people have been taught to breathe in exactly the opposite manner!

There are two effective ways for beginners to observe and control their breathing:

- *Counting. You can choose to count to four or six on the inhale and the same measure on the exhale, making sure to keep a natural rhythm. By counting, you are in essence also performing a mantra or meditation, which takes your mind off other worries.*
- *Following. Once your breathing takes on a natural rhythm, you can move beyond counting and simply follow the pattern — in, out, in, out. If you do this for five minutes, you will immediately notice that your stress level drops and your mind develops a much-needed clarity.*

3. One-pointed meditation

One-pointed meditation is, as the name implies, bringing your mind into focus by concentrating on a single object: a flower, a color, a pen, or a pebble. Some practitioners prefer to visualize the object with their eyes closed, whereas for others it is more effective to perform the meditation with their eyes open.

Either way, the point is that when your mind is focused on the object, it should be relaxed. However, if it is too relaxed there is a danger of your thoughts wandering or of sleepiness. You should have a moderate degree of intensity while maintaining single-pointedness, as though your mind has fused with the chosen object. This unusual combination of intensity and relaxed alertness is essential. The image should be both clear and stable in your mind. Laurens writes:

> *Anant Asavabhokin, CEO of Land & Houses Ltd. in Thailand, explained to me that he chooses a beautiful image of a mountain, the sea, or a landscape and concentrates on that.*
>
> *At the end of a two-week session with the Dalai Lama, His Holiness presented me with a wonderful statue of Buddha that I have on my desk. When I do one-pointed meditation, I try to remember the statue in minute detail. According to Buddhist instructions, you should try to see the object in your mind as vividly and luminously as possible. That for me has been quite difficult, but when I succeed, I feel peace afterward.*

4. Analytical meditation

The purpose of analytical meditation is to strengthen your ability to analyze a subject from many different perspectives and to concentrate on this subject for long periods of time. Analytical meditation involves using reasoning skills[5] to bring about inner change through systematic investigation and analysis. In this way you can properly use your human intelligence—your capacity for reason and analysis—to contribute to your level of understanding about life. I should point out that the difference between one-pointed and analytical meditation is not the type of subject or object on which you choose to focus. The difference lies in how your mind is directed.

Take, for example, a negative emotion such as anger. When practicing analytical meditation, you begin by reflecting on the destructive effects of anger on your physical health and emotional relationships. You analyze and reflect on it not just once or twice but repeatedly, until it becomes part of your deeper understanding. Now the next time someone harms you, your immediate response is still to become angry. But when the emotion of anger arises, you remember from your meditation the destructive nature of anger, and that immediately makes you more conscious of the undesirability of giving in to anger and letting it escalate within you. And through this process you are able to gain control over your mind and let go of the negative emotion.

This doesn't mean you shouldn't try to prevent people from harming you. On the contrary, you should take measures to prevent harm to yourself and others. But despite your best efforts, harm will sometimes occur, and using this kind of meditation can help defuse the intensity of your anger, allowing you to respond to the situation without feeling hatred.

You may have committed harmful acts in the past that you regret, but these do not necessarily make you a permanently bad person. You can learn to separate another person's harmful actions from that person as a totality. Remind yourself that perhaps there are other factors at play that you are not aware of that may have caused the person to act in the way he or she did. With practice, you can also analyze the situation from a wider

perspective and even try to discover if this harmful act or difficult situation might be used in some way to enhance your spiritual growth, taken as an opportunity to make you stronger.

Another example of analytical meditation is developing ap-
preciation of the efforts and kindness of others. Meditating on
the value of kindness is a worthy effort. Our survival depends
entirely on others. Having food depends on others; acquiring
clothing depends on others; and obtaining housing depends on
others. You may think, "I paid for all these things," but that
money did not come out of thin air; it depended on others. Then
you may feel, "Yes, these are facts, but the others did not deliberately help me. They did it as a by-product of their efforts to
survive." That is true. But I cherish many things that do not return my concern. For example, if my watch fell on the floor and
broke, I would feel a loss. That does not mean that this watch has
some feeling for me. It is useful to me, so I care about it. In the
same way, all those people may not have done anything for us
deliberately, but as their work is useful for us, we should recognize their contribution. We depend on their contribution and
their efforts for our own survival. Thinking along these lines will
change your attitude.

Analytical meditation can be applied not just to negative emotions, but to any concept of which you are trying to gain a better
understanding. For example, if you wanted to develop a deeper
comprehension of a difficult concept like "impermanence," you
would make it the focus of your meditation and examine the concept from all perspectives: as it applies to living things, dead
things, and both short-term and long-term aspects of life. You
would consider it in relation to different phenomena within the
worlds of science, music, business, even happiness.[6] This type of

meditation can be particularly useful for decision making in business because it can help leaders gain a deeper and more profound understanding of complex concepts or situations.

VISUALIZATION EXERCISES

Visualization exercises involve some more advanced control over the mind. This type of meditation asks you to imagine yourself changing into something else, and its purpose for non-Buddhists is to calm the mind. Here is just one example of how to go about it.[7]

Imagine that you have three channels in your body. The central channel is a transparent tube about the width of your little finger, running straight down the center of your body from the crown of your head to the base of your spine. The right and the left channels are also transparent tubes but are narrower than the central channel. They run from your nostrils up to the crown of your head, where they curve down like an umbrella handle to run along the central channel, parallel with the spine to slightly below your navel, where they join the central channel.

Having visualized these three channels, first breathe in through your left nostril, imagining that the air is flowing into the crown of your head and continuing down the left channel to the level of your navel, where it switches to the right channel. Here, you breathe out through that channel, the air passing the crown of the head and flowing out past the right nostril. Repeat this three times. Next, do the same exercise, starting with the air coming in through the right nostril and going out though the left nostril. Do this three times. Lastly, breathe in through both nostrils together, visualizing bringing the air past the crown and down through the right and left channels to the point where they join the central channel. When the air reaches the central channel, tighten your inner pelvis and hold your breath. As soon as you no longer feel comfortable, exhale naturally through your nostrils, but visualize that, instead of the air going out, it dissolves inside the central channel. Do this three times.

Being skeptical by nature, when I read how to do this exercise for the first time, my reaction was that it was absolute nonsense. But the Buddha teaches that you should not believe anything until you have experienced it yourself and have made extensive verification based on your own experience. One of the most helpful descriptions of this attitude is presented by Piet Hut, an astrophysicist and professor at Princeton University, in his article "Life as a Laboratory."[8] Hut writes:

> After decades during which it was extremely un-popular among scientists to even mention the word "religion" I have seen many colleagues coming "out of the closet," as I have myself, by attending meetings and writing papers on the general topic of science and deeply felt human experience, with a nod to spirituality. I have started to view life as a laboratory, as an opportunity to examine ourselves and our world.

I found that Hut's view really hit home, and I decided to give visualization a try. When I returned home from India after living for two weeks in a tent with very rudimentary

*facilities, my family expected me to be in bad shape. To
their surprise, I was perhaps a little thinner but in
excellent spirits. The meditation had achieved the desired
effect; it had calmed my mind.*

5. Citing mantras

Citing mantras is considered a more advanced form of meditation and does not come naturally to some people. Its purpose is
again to calm the mind. In fact, the roots of the word "mantra"
are "manna," which means "mind," and "tra," which means "protection."[9] Buddhists believe that citing a mantra, a sequence of
words, can help to protect the mind from negative thoughts and
emotions. We also believe that it is good for spiritual development.

Many different mantras exist for different purposes. For instance, when someone is focusing on developing a good heart,
they concentrate on the mantra Om Mani Padme Hum. This
mantra is also often recited as a dedication when someone has
died. When my mother passed away, my brother and I and many
others recited Om Mani Padme Hum more than a hundred
thousand times.

The meaning of Om Mani Padme Hum is very inspiring.[10]
"Om," pronounced "aum" or "ohm," means "body, speech, and
mind." When we use the sound "om," it signifies that we would
like to develop a pure body, speech, and mind, like those of
Buddha. Purity, here, refers to the absence of negative thoughts
and emotions and of bad (unwholesome) actions. The remaining
syllables indicate how to make this transition and use objects
as symbols. "Mani," meaning "jewel," relates to Right Conduct,

taking the right action inspired by an altruistic intention. "Padme" means "lotus." A lotus is perfectly white even though it grows out of mud, and so it represents how a mind that is impure (stained with mud) can become pure (perfectly white) by taking the Right View. "Hum" means "indivisible," that is, that Right View and Right Conduct must be combined (see chapters 1 and 2).

Part 2

[Leading Your Organization]

It is the task of the leader to create a company

with a strong and warm heart

and to see things as they really are.

4

The Leader's Purpose

As the head of the Tibetan government-in-exile, I visit Tibetans all over the world who always give me a very hearty welcome. This is in part because I see one of my most important tasks as giving Tibetans faith in the future. I am surprised how strong that faith can be. Even though many live in miserable circumstances outside Tibet, they have remained a faithful and optimistic people.

Whether you are a spiritual leader or a leader in an organization, it is your job to inspire faith. But a leader who inspires faith has to be very careful about engendering the right kind of faith. He or she should be honest and not demand blind faith. In the Buddhist tradition, we think that it is essential to combine faith with wisdom. Wisdom in this context means Right View, which we know means seeing the way things really are and understanding impermanence, interdependence, and dependent origination. Faith needs support—and this support comes from wisdom.

The wise leader examines the cause and effect of an objective or event, whether it is correct, appropriate, true, or false. If faith stands alone, it is prone to deception and errors of judgment and is easily influenced by emotion. Without wisdom we may believe whatever people tell us, no matter whether what they say is right or wrong. Faith may give us strength to do anything, even something evil. When faith is so strong, I remind people to keep it under the control of wisdom, so as to stay in proper balance.

Unfortunately, many leaders in business today lack wisdom and fail to inspire faith in those they lead. The goal of this chapter is to help you, as a leader, to inspire faith in your employees and your organization.

> *Many people feel that we do not have the right leaders, either in business or in government, and we certainly have many bad leaders. Inadequate leadership at the level of companies results in business scandals, which leads to businesses as a group having a poor reputation. Inadequate leadership at the level of countries results in poverty and war.*
>
> *One significant problem is that people feel a lack of fairness. In prosperous countries this comes about as a consequence of an increase in inequality and growing insecurity about jobs; in developing and poor countries people are conscious of social injustice to an unprecedented degree and resentful of their deprivation and lack of personal dignity. They hold their leaders responsible, both corporate and national.*
>
> *Another major challenge is that leaders must be able to deal with crises. Increasing interdependence has two opposite effects: the system can deal more effectively with*

some shocks, but a small shock in one part can have disastrous consequences in others. One example can be seen in the fallout from the problems in the U.S. subprime mortgage market at the end of 2007. The fact that lenders sold loans to people who could not afford them, and the subsequent packaging of those mortgages into various investment vehicles that later became nearly worthless due to the high level of foreclosures, led to losses estimated to be at least $200 billion in major financial institutions worldwide. Given the interdependence of complex systems such as these, a leader must have the ability to maintain a calm, collected, and concentrated mind in a crisis.

The challenges are growing in importance and urgency. To meet them, leaders have to improve the performance of their minds. Following Right View and Right Conduct can make an important contribution in this. For example, if the people inside the company feel that they are respected and appreciated, that hiring and promotion practices are based on merit without any discrimination, they will perceive the company as fair. The same applies to customers, if an organization demonstrates a genuine interest in their well-being and if its business practices are shown to be equitable.

Whether you are a leader in a four-person company, a multinational conglomerate, or a government office, the first step in restoring faith among those you lead is to inspire them with a sense of purpose—just as His Holiness has done for thousands of displaced Tibetans all over the world. In this chapter, we explain how a leader can establish a clear purpose for the company and set values that should be observed by all.

Defining the Purpose of the Organization

In his classic book, Dilemmas of Leadership in the Democratic Process, *Chester Barnard wrote about the tasks of the leader,*[1] *and his characterization still stands. He saw that a leader's job is to formulate and define purpose; provide a system of communication; attract and retain competent people; and encourage them to put their best efforts into realizing the purpose of the business.*

That sounds straightforward enough. So why is it that true leadership eludes so many? Because effective leadership requires the ability to build faith — and not everyone has that gift. Barnard comments:

> *Leadership must inspire cooperative decision making by creating faith: faith in the common understanding, faith in the probability of ultimate success, faith in the ultimate satisfaction of personal motives, faith in the integrity of the leadership, faith in the superiority of the common purpose of the organization as a personal aim of its members. Without the creation of faith, the catalyst by which the living system of human efforts is enabled to continue its incessant interchanges of energy and satisfactions, vitality will be lacking and the company will die.*

In other words, an essential element of good leadership is being able to clarify the organization's purpose, often a remarkably difficult task. Without a meaningful and achievable purpose, however, it is impossible to attain a high level of morale and right motivation within a company. People like—in fact they need—to know the purpose of what they are doing.

The importance of having a clear purpose was described very effectively by Jim Collins in his bestseller Good to Great.[2] *Collins compared "great" companies with others in the same industrial sectors: great companies are defined by having much better performance (measured in shareholder value) over a period of fifteen years. He found that it often took even great companies more than a year to define their purpose and several years to implement it. In fact, in most cases a competent top management team had to be fully in place before a purpose could be effectively enacted. Without leaders who believe in that purpose, communicate it, follow it, and make sure that employees work in accordance with it, motivation, and therefore productivity, falls flat.*

In many companies, the purpose is referred to as the "mission." Jack Welch, retired CEO of GE, recently found that, to his surprise, 60 percent of CEOs attending his seminars did not have a company mission statement, and 80 percent had no explicit set of company values. On top of that, he found that many mission statements were empty and meaningless, like "Our mission is to be the best company in the industry." Good leaders present a clear, precise, and meaningful statement of their company's purpose. A good example of this is Google's mission statement: "To organize the world's information and make it universally accessible and useful."[3]

If you ask people what their purpose in life is, very few have a clear answer. But many do have at least some idea of what their purpose is at work. This shared purpose is a precondition for people who want to identify with their organization. If they find out, after joining the company, that they do not like its purpose or that it has no clear purpose at all, they will be disappointed and unhappy in their jobs. But if their leaders inspire in them a clear sense of purpose, they will be fulfilled and motivated, which will contribute to their overall happiness.

Establishing Values

Once you have clarified your organization's purpose, one of your next responsibilities as a leader is to define the values and principles that management and employees will adhere to when making decisions. Such statements of values go by many names, such as "codes of ethics," "codes of conduct," or "corporate responsibility statements."

Clearly, it is up to leaders to create these kinds of statements and to act according to their principles. Therefore, the principles have to be established under the direct leadership of the chief executive, not delegated to anyone else.

Cor Herkströter, former CEO of Shell and present chairman of ING, reveals that these principles are immensely difficult to formulate. He comments that the value of principles increases enormously when they are never changed; principles that are changed from year to year become valueless to employees and, in turn, to the company. But, as he tells me, "Once the principles have the right quality, people will say, 'That's it, I could have written that myself.'"

   Herkströter explains that a company's principles should:

- *Be clear and easy to understand*
- *Appeal to the people working for the company*
- *Help people to make responsible decisions*
- *Be meaningful in different cultures (for a global company)*

In addition to creating a corporate code of conduct, a strong leader should also have a clear view of the company's "corporate citizenship," how the company will act as a responsible member of society (much as an individual citizen should). Many different names have been given to this concept, including "sustainability," "corporate social responsibility (CSR)," and "triple bottom line."

   No matter the term, one could say that corporate citizenship is the application of the Buddhist concepts of Right View and Right Conduct to companies instead of to individuals. For instance, most companies, when defining their values, use the idea of a "stakeholder." A stakeholder is not simply a financial investor, but, when used in the context of corporate citizenship, incorporates all the individuals and organizations affected by the actions of the company. That includes an inner circle of employees, shareholders, customers, and suppliers, as well as many other organizations in the industry and the communities where the company operates. (The environment is also affected by the actions of a company.) As a result, it is important that a company's values and principles fit with the concept of Right Conduct.

The Dalai Lama offers a number of good examples of corporate values and principles that Laurens presented to him:

- We expect all our employees to act with honesty, integrity, and fairness.
- We will help the people of the world to have fuller lives—both through the services we provide and through the impact we have on the world around us.
- We accept our responsibility to engage with communities, and we will invest in society in a way that makes effective use of our resources, including supporting charitable organizations.
- We are committed to sustainable business practices and environmental protection.
- Our customers have chosen to trust us. In return, we must strive to anticipate and understand their needs and delight them with our service.

The Leader's Character

So the main tasks of a leader are clarifying purpose, defining values, building faith, and making the right decisions. And most people would agree that the quality of an organization's leadership is the greatest predictor of its success. So what kind of person makes the best kind of leader? One with character.

It is important to distinguish between "technical" skills and character, as Chester Barnard wrote:

> *A leader should have superior technical skills in understanding technology, in perception, in knowledge, in memory, in imagination. He should also have above average levels of determination, endurance, and courage.*[5]

The Dalai Lama explains that one can build character by applying the principles of Right View and Right Conduct. Buddhism offers a list of "seven character traits of an ideal person" that all of us should strive for if we want to lead with character.

1. Understanding principles and causes

Leaders with character are aware of the duties and responsibilities of their role and of the challenges they face. Leaders should be able to identify the causes of problems and the principles that should be applied to solve them.

2. Understanding objectives and results

Leaders know the meaning and objectives of the principles they abide by; they understand the tasks they are undertaking; they understand the reasons behind their actions. They know what may be expected in the future as a result of their actions and whether these will lead to a good or bad result. This kind of foresight is important for leaders when they are considering the long-term effects of their decisions on others.

3. Understanding themselves

Leaders know their strengths, aptitudes, abilities, and virtues and are able to correct and improve themselves. They are also aware of their weaknesses and the weaknesses of the company, and how the company, in turn, affects its many stakeholder groups. They must be very eager to learn.

4. Understanding moderation

Leaders practice moderation in speech, work, and action. They do not take unnecessary actions merely to satisfy their own egos or accomplish their own ends, but take only those actions that will benefit the organization for which they are responsible.

5. Understanding the occasion and efficient use of time

Leaders know the proper occasion for actions—what should be done and how—and they perform these actions efficiently. This includes knowing how to plan their time and organize it effectively. Additionally, leaders must have "discernment," the ability to identify the issues that matter most and concentrate on them. It is very important to avoid wasting time on trivial matters.

6. Understanding the organization

Leaders know that organizations have rules and regulations; they have a culture and traditions; people within them have individual needs that should be dealt with, helped along, and served in the proper way. Good leaders understand not only their own character, but the character of the company and their responsibility for developing and nurturing that character, and they should be aware if some aspect of the character needs to be changed.

7. *Understanding people*

Leaders know and comprehend differences among individuals. They know how to relate to people effectively, what can be learned from them, and how they should be praised, criticized, advised, and taught.

Leadership with a Trained Mind

Hundreds of books have been written about the characteristics of leaders and on how people can train themselves to become "great" leaders. All these books present different prescriptions. But the fact is, no two leaders are exactly alike, and no one can become a great leader just by following a particular recipe. However, the Dalai Lama is convinced that if an individual with the right potential learns to think and act with a trained mind, his or her performance will greatly improve.

People who have never experienced the reality of being a leader often do not realize how demanding the job is. When I was promoted to president of the company for which I worked, I was extremely happy. But soon thereafter I realized the difficulties, endless conflicts between people, dissatisfied clients, and unfavorable currency fluctuations I was facing, and I was losing good

people and working eighteen hours a day. The most
difficult problems always end up on the leader's desk. And
that is the way it should be. My point is that being a leader
is very hard work, which is why a leader must develop the
capability to cope with the inevitable ups and downs by
maintaining a calm, collected, and concentrated mind
under all circumstances, however adverse.

Buddhist teachings contain innumerable lists on how to
train the mind to cope with different problems. We have
selected one that is particularly relevant for leaders, called
the Eight Worldly Concerns. These are about states or
events that happen to all of us: criticism, praise, failure,
success, making money, losing money, being famous, and
not receiving any recognition whatsoever. The Dalai Lama
offers a simple explanation of these concerns, as well as
advice for coping with them.

The Eight Worldly Concerns are presented in what appears to be a conflicting way, but this is deliberate. They consist of four pairs that appear to be contradictory:

- Becoming distressed when someone insults or belittles you
- Becoming elated when someone praises you
- Feeling depressed when you experience failure
- Feeling happy when you experience success
- Being dispirited when you become poor
- Being joyful when you acquire wealth
- Feeling upset when you lack recognition
- Feeling pleased when you achieve fame

The first concern, becoming distressed when someone belittles you, appears to be just as natural as becoming elated when someone praises you. But in fact, although it seems natural, it is the wrong reaction for someone with a trained mind. When a person with an untrained mind is belittled, he or she becomes unhappy or angry. The person with a trained mind reacts differently. He or she asks him- or herself: "What is the motivation of the person who is belittling me? Is this person competent to hold an opinion? Is the opinion justified?" If it is justified, there is something to learn and one should explain that one unfortunately made a mistake. If the opinion is not justified, and the other person is acting out of malice, someone with a trained mind will see this as an opportunity to test his or her ability to stay calm.

The same process should be followed when being praised. What is the motivation of the person giving the praise? Is the praise being given by a person who understands what has been accomplished? Is the person's judgment valuable, or does he or she merely want to please or, worse, flatter because he or she desires something in return? Praise and criticism alike have to be dispassionately evaluated for what they are worth. The objective is not to avoid criticism or to get praise—it is to learn from your mistakes or your accomplishments.

The reasoning is the same with the other pairs. Feeling depressed when you experience failure is as natural as feeling happy when you experience success. However, being depressed is a negative emotion; it does not have a positive value. Instead of increasing one's energy to solve a problem, it leaves one with less. Therefore, a person with a trained mind will analyze whether the failure is due to mistakes or to external circumstances. If it is diagnosed as a mistake, that person will ask him- or herself if anything can be learned in order to avoid similar failures in the future.

On the other hand, being elated by success does not have the negative consequence of reducing energy. Instead, it increases positive energy. But the danger lies in believing that the success was entirely due to your own brilliance and that the success of all future actions is therefore certain. Every successful outcome is the result of many factors coming together. Your decision or action may have been only one of many. It is important to reflect on the contributions other people have made and the other circumstances that made the success possible. Believing that you will be successful in everything you do is dangerous because it can lead to arrogance and false pride, which in turn leads to poor decisions.

The third pair is also perfectly natural—being dispirited when you become poor and joyful when you acquire wealth. Nobody acts with the intention of becoming poor. Or in business terminology, no business intends to suffer a loss. But the reality is that many businesses occasionally do lose money. Becoming dispirited when that happens is of no use. The right frame of mind is to figure out how the losses can be changed into profits.

Similarly, being joyful when the company is successful, including making good profits, is natural. The risk is seeing the success as something permanent. Unless the right decisions are made, even the most profitable company may eventually lose money. Therefore, being happy is fine as long as it does not lead to thinking that a company that does not change will remain successful.

Being pleased with fame can be the result of seeking fame. Fame is like wealth: it can easily lead to an insatiable desire for more. The first problem is that someone with an insatiable desire for fame will never be happy, as fame will always be limited. There will always be people who are more famous. The second point is that fame is only fine when it is the result of Right Action. It is bad when it is sought for its own sake, without regard for the right actions. It requires considerable effort for an ambitious person not to become addicted to fame.

Clearly, there is a pattern here: one should celebrate joyful events while not becoming too attached to their meaning, either in the present or as a predictor of the future. Laurens offers the following example from the workplace:

> *A CEO of a leading software company learns that she has been selected as one of the best one hundred managers of the year. She feels pleased, as well she should. (If she had been listed as one of the worst, she'd naturally be unhappy.) The managers who are not on the list think that they should have been selected and are jealous. (Others, who were afraid they might be chosen as one of the worst, are happy that they are not on the list.) These reactions are natural. This CEO has a trained mind and Right View, and so she is pleased to have been selected but will also reflect on the help she received from others—and on the role of luck.*
>
> *A CEO from another company, on the other hand, learns he has not made it onto this list. He too has a trained mind, so he first takes time to calm down, because it is unavoidable that he will be unhappy. Though he realizes that the people in his company, as well as his friends and family, will read about it, he understands that getting angry and blaming others or the magazine is a*

waste of mental energy. So he reflects on whether there is any justification in his not being selected and whether there are lessons to be learned. He knows that taking Right View means learning to direct his mind in a constructive way, especially when the ego has been hurt.

Nita Ing, chief executive of Continental Engineering in Taiwan, told me about an important event in her life that came about once she learned to apply Right View. She is chairwoman of the Taiwan High-Speed Rail Corporation (THSRC), which bid for the $15 billion contract to build a high-speed train system in Taiwan. The consortium she was bidding against had close links to the government in power, while Ing supported the head of the opposition party. When the bids were opened, THSRC's bid was substantially better. It is not hard to imagine the government's dismay at having to award the largest contract in Taiwanese history to a consortium led by a woman supporting the opposition.

As might be expected, a campaign was launched to change the outcome. Tax inspectors were sent in to check Continental Engineering's accounts in an attempt to find illegal activity such as tax evasion. Ing and her children were threatened. The media began to depict her as too incompetent to handle such a large contract. It all became too much for her to bear. An independently wealthy woman, she questioned why she should ruin her life and those of her children just to win a contract.

Ing informed her Buddhism teacher that she was going to quit the following day. Her teacher, Zopa Rinpoche,[6] said, "You must do what you think is right, but think about the fact that the project you are involved in is a great gift."

Ing's reaction was, "A gift? You cannot be serious — it is destroying me."

Her teacher answered, "It is a great gift because it gives you a great opportunity to achieve change for the better. Please do one thing for me: think about it. And calm down. Do not make a decision when you are upset, because you do not see things the way they really are."

After some hesitation, Ing decided to follow his advice. She thought about her decision overnight and did not quit — and her consortium won the contract.

Developing Mindfulness

Applying Right View, especially mindfulness, is particularly important for a business leader. Say a CEO has called a meeting of senior executives to discuss an important issue for which everyone's input is needed. The meeting is to start at ten o'clock. When the CEO arrives at that time, he notices (feeling) that one of his executives is not there (perception and consciousness). He now has several options to choose from: waiting until the missing person arrives, starting the meeting anyway, calling the person on his mobile phone, or calling his secretary to find out why the person is not there. For the untrained person this process has an emotional dimension. The CEO feels annoyed that the executive has not shown up. He may see it as a lack of discipline or a lack of respect for him and for the other participants, who have all come on time. He might well become angry, especially if the missing person is often late—a typical example of how negative thoughts and emotions arise.

These all seem like natural reactions, but recognize that people with an untrained mind often misinterpret the situation. In the cycle of feeling, perception, and consciousness, they instantly classify a feeling into categories: like or do not like, friendly or unfriendly, positive or negative, and so on.

On the flip side, the person with a trained mind learns how to avoid this instant classification. Making the right choice depends on seeing reality, being able to generate constructive solutions, and making decisions with a calm and collected mind. The Buddhist method for making calm and collected decisions involves asking ourselves four questions:

1. What is the reality and is it a problem?
2. What is the cause of the problem?
3. What do I want to achieve?
4. How can I arrive at the goal?

Let's return to our example and consider a potential response after thinking it through in the right way. When the senior manager does not arrive on time to the meeting, the person with the trained mind will not get upset or angry or worried. First he will find out why the manager was late. Then he will determine what he wants to accomplish in his response, and he will analyze the best way to achieve that goal.

Here, a person with a trained mind will consider the

situation from different perspectives. How important is it that everyone arrive on time to meetings? What are the consequences of the different actions he could take? Are others in the meeting bothered by this person's lateness? Might there be acceptable reasons for a person being late, like being stuck on the phone with one of the company's most important clients?

If the CEO concludes that a late arrival to an important meeting is a serious problem, he will think about how he can change the behavior of people who are often late. What he will not do is show anger toward the senior manager who was late, because a person with a trained mind has learned that getting angry is unlikely to solve the problem. If he thinks it is a serious problem, he will raise the issue calmly with the person.

If you can learn to recognize when your feelings are getting in the way of seeing reality, you will be able to make better business decisions. This is developing mindfulness.

If an organization seeks out leaders who exhibit the qualities described in this book, it will be placing its trust in those who put the well-being of the organization as a whole above all other considerations. Many leaders in the modern-day corporate environment do not think this way. In fact, some think the opposite: they believe they should maintain distance from their employees and be shrewd and heartless in the face of tough decision making. What leaders should in fact focus on is the need to satisfy employees, customers, and shareholders. This can be done through a variety of means, many of them financial, but it also requires maintaining a good reputation and a high level of motivation in the organization. Leaders who possess the characteristics described in this book will be able to meet these objectives by having a clear purpose and applying wisdom.

Continuity of Leadership

Given the vital role that a leader plays in a company, appointing the right person is one of the most important considerations. This is the responsibility of the board of directors. When looking for a successor to an incumbent chief executive, the best solution may be to appoint someone who is already working for the company. Such a person is already known by the board members, employees, and other stakeholders. The challenge for the company is to have a succession-planning system in place that identifies people with the potential to become leaders and develops their competences and skills systematically.

Unfortunately, the majority of companies do not have such a system. Why? It is a problem of lack of courage. Board members find it uncomfortable to talk to the current chief executive about who should replace him (or her) if he leaves. Most chief executives love their jobs and if they had the choice would postpone their retirement indefinitely. Therefore, many show only a lukewarm interest in succession planning.

Someone from outside the company carries a much higher risk when appointed to a CEO position and may well have to be paid much more than an insider. The importance of payment should not be underestimated. Many insiders are very keen to get such a job, even with only a small increment over their current pay. An outsider may have to be paid double that amount. Apart from this increase for one person, doing so would pull up the compensation of other members of top management, so the total extra costs are far higher than just the increase in compensation for the outsider. Nevertheless, even in companies with a succession-planning system, an outsider may have to be chosen if none of the internal candidates is suitable, and there may be circumstances when "fresh blood" is a benefit, particularly in times of change.

There are few board decisions more important than making sure that competent successors are selected as heads of companies. In this chapter we have described the characteristics boards should be looking for. We have also indicated that these characteristics can be developed and should therefore be part of skills development for potential leaders.

Working on this book has helped me to realize how complicated the role of a corporate leader is. As a result, I have become even more convinced that leaders need to develop a holistic view of business. In the past it may have been enough for a leader to concentrate on leading the people in his or her organization. This is no longer the case. Today, a leader must also engage with the wider world. In doing so, businesses hold the potential to solve many of the world's problems. That is what the final section of this book is all about. For this engagement to be effective, the leader must try to understand the very different ways of thinking of these other groups. Adversarial relationships are to be avoided, so in this context humility is very important. These other groups often understand very little about the world of business, and they may have many beliefs that do not correspond to reality. It is the task of the leader to help them find the "truth." An arrogant attitude will have negative consequences. Patience and respect for others are essential. The people appointing the successor should keep this in the back of their minds at all times: This person will be responsible for providing the company with a strong and warm heart. Can he or she do that?

My own succession is also of great concern to me. This is complicated, because a definite and final solution can be established only after the government in China recognizes and accepts that the establishment of Tibet as a genuine autonomous region within China is the only and best solution for China and for the Tibetans. My health is very good, and I hope that this will happen in my lifetime. But as a responsible leader, I have to prepare for the eventuality that it will happen only after my death. The Right View is impermanence, and therefore a change in the attitudes of the Chinese government is inevitable. While the Chinese government has already reduced restrictions on religious freedom since the 1980s, it is impossible to predict when the right attitude change concerning Tibet will occur.

Right action in this situation requires patience and skill. I have therefore decided to examine with the most senior members of the Tibetan community how to organize my succession, in case a change in attitude by the Chinese government comes too late. We will select the most capable man or woman, acceptable to and fully supported by the Tibetan people and the religious leaders in Tibetan Buddhism, to provide continuity of leadership after my death. That is my duty.

5

The Role
of an Organization:
Creating Profit,
Jobs — or Happiness?

Any organization is both more and less than the sum of its members. It is less because the members of the group devote only a part of their time to the organization and more because the organization as a whole can accomplish tasks the individual members cannot succeed in carrying out on their own.

The other day, when I was traveling from the railway station in Pathankot to where I live in Dharamsala, the car was halted because woodsmen were cutting down a tree that was at risk of falling onto the road. After the tree was felled, two skinny old men began to saw the trunk into pieces so that the road could be cleared. As you can imagine, an ever-growing number of cars began to line up on both sides of the tree. Many people got out of their cars to watch the two men struggling with their saw. There must have been more than one hundred people watching the two men work. Then one of the spectators came forward and with a wave of his arm invited other people to join him in pushing the tree to the side of the road. In less than five minutes, twenty men had moved the tree and the traffic obstruction was removed.

This so simply demonstrated what people can do when they cooperate. It also demonstrated to me the power of initiative; if nobody had taken the initiative to start the cooperative effort, we would all have had to wait more than two hours before we could have continued. The people moving the tree were not a business—they did not even know one another—but they had a common purpose, and a leader who took the initiative to articulate that purpose and find a way to solve the problem.

> If part of the role of the leader is to clarify purpose and inspire faith in organizational goals and values, as outlined in chapter 4, then what role does the organization as a whole play? Is the real purpose of business simply to make a profit—to "maximize shareholder value"—or is there something larger at stake? Of course, business leaders will argue that profit is paramount; otherwise, a company cannot survive. That is true, **but more forward-thinking leaders recognize that when working together toward a common purpose, businesses and organizations can also achieve other admirable goals.**
>
> In 1977, professor Peter Drucker commented:
>
>> A business cannot be defined or explained in terms of profit. Asked what a business is, the typical businessman is likely to answer, "an organization to make profit." The typical economist is likely to give the same answer. This answer is not only false; it is

irrelevant. The concept of profit maximization is, in fact, meaningless. Profitability is not the purpose of, but the limiting factor on, business enterprise. Profit is not the explanation, cause, or rationale of business decisions, but a test of their validity. The purpose of a business must lie outside the business itself. In fact, it must lie in society, since business enterprise is an organ of society.

Dhaldol Bunnag, the Buddhist CEO of AIG Thailand, offers an additional way to see the role of the organization:

> *For me, the purpose of my business is to build a team of successful people with high morale, good attitudes, and good faith. Building the agency force to sell insurance is to teach them to bring benefits to others. Profits are just an end result, rather than the purpose of business.*

Buddhist scholar Venerable P. A. Payutto agrees:

> *From the Buddhist point of view, economic activity should be a means to a good and noble life. Production, consumption and other economic activities are not ends in themselves; they are means, and the end to which they must lead is the development of well-being within the individual, within society and within the environment.[1]*

The Buddhist View of Profit

In the Buddhist tradition we have a very clear view of profit—that it is a fine aim (as long as it has been earned honestly) but that it is not the purpose of business. To say that the role of business is to make a profit makes as much sense as to say that the role of a person is to eat or to breathe. If a company loses money, it dies, as does a person without food or oxygen, but that does not mean that profit is the business's sole purpose for being.

My preference would be for businesses to define their goals in terms of meeting the needs of their customers (while acting responsibly), rather than making money or maximizing shareholder value alone. Sure, acting responsibly includes making a healthy profit to ensure the livelihood of employees and deliver satisfactory increases in shareholder value. But making profit the single most important objective is not only at odds with Buddhist philosophy. It is dangerous to the organization.

Certainly, employees do not want to work for a company that is losing money, for that imperils their job security. On the other hand, they want to work for a company of which they can be proud, a company that has a solid reputation as a supplier of high-quality, useful products and services. That is why defining the organization's role in a motivating and positive way is very important.

Creating Wealth

Wealth is obviously important for business, and wealth can be an important force for good. It is the product of work, and in

Buddhism work is considered to be very important. According to Buddhist teachings, a person's first responsibility is to take care of him- or herself, and next to help others. So striving to create wealth is not at all at odds with Buddhist philosophy, as long as that wealth is not used improperly.

The Improper Use of Wealth

Wealth can be used for good, but it can also be used the wrong way, to harmful ends, such as with corruption. Buddhism also considers hoarding wealth to be using it improperly. The following story illustrates this point.

The Buddha was once visited by Pasenadi, King of Kosala. The king explained that a wealthy man had just died and had left no instructions regarding the disbursement of his property. Therefore, Pasenadi had ordered that the goods be brought to the royal residence. The deceased had always dressed in very poor garments and had been in the habit of eating only sour husk gruel, yet when the goods arrived, they included vast quantities of gold and silver. This man had not utilized his wealth properly—he had used it neither to take care of himself nor to care for his parents, wife, children, workers, or friends. So the ruler confiscated it and distributed it to heirs for whom the deceased had displayed no regard.[2]

The Buddha confirmed that this would have been the natural order of events and that in the opposite circumstances, if the wealthy man had allocated his wealth properly, he would have been happier himself, he would have made others happy, and his charitable deeds and almsgiving would have left a happy memory. His riches would not have been wasted. Both

the squandering and the hoarding of wealth are therefore de-
plored.

In Buddhism, we think a great deal about death, the importance of accepting death as an inevitable fact, and the desir-
ability of dying satisfied with what one has done. In the above
story, it is almost certain that the person died alone without anybody at his side and suffered because he had to abandon his
wealth.

Becoming Wealthy in the Right Way

Buddha taught that *how* a person earns wealth is just as important as how he or she uses it. He wrote:

> Good and praiseworthy people are those who seek
> wealth in rightful ways and use it for the good and hap-
> piness of both themselves and others.[3]

A parable ascribed to Buddha describes this concept in further detail:

> Monks, there are three groups of people in this world.
> What are these three? They are the blind, the one-eyed,
> and the two-eyed. Who is the blind person? There are
> some in this world who do not have the vision that
> leads to the acquisition of wealth or to the increase of
> wealth already gained. Moreover, they do not have the
> vision that enables them to know what actions lead to
> positive results, and the ones that do not, they do not
> know what deserves disapproval, what is vulgar, and

what is refined, good and evil. That is what I mean by the one that is blind.

Who is the one-eyed person? These people have the vision to acquire wealth but are otherwise the same as the blind person. This I call a one-eyed person. And who is the two-eyed person? These people have the vision to acquire wealth and capitalize on it, have the vision that enables them to know what actions lead to positive results, and the ones that do not, what deserves disapproval and what not, what is vulgar and what is refined, good and evil. This I call the person with two eyes.

The one who is blind is hounded by misfortune on two counts: he has no wealth, and he performs no good works.

The second kind of person, the one-eyed, looks about for wealth irrespective of whether it is right or wrong. It may be obtained through theft, cheating or fraud. He enjoys pleasures of the senses from his ability to acquire wealth. The one-eyed person suffers according to his deeds.

The two-eyed person is a fine human being, one who shares out a portion of the wealth obtained through his diligent labor. He has noble thoughts, a resolute mind and will be free of suffering. Avoid the blind and the one-eyed, and associate with the two-eyed.[4]

This parable is very relevant for businesspeople. Leaders must have vision to create wealth and also know the right and proper ways to earn and use that wealth. Good business leaders know what actions are disreputable and can distinguish between wrong and right. The story also expresses the Buddhist view that a good businessperson will be happy: "He . . . will be free from suffering."

"The one-eyed person . . . enjoys pleasures of the senses from his ability to acquire wealth" can be misunderstood without an explanation. "Enjoying the senses" in Buddhist texts can have two meanings, positive and negative. For example, there is nothing wrong with enjoying a good meal. But the parable refers to a person who is vulgar and does not know what is refined. He may therefore become addicted to good food, eat too much, and grow obese. He may be unhappy when he has to eat a simple but healthy meal. There are many other such addictions, like gambling, drinking too much, and so on.

"The one-eyed person suffers according to his deeds" refers to the Buddhist belief that a person who acts badly will suffer. I realize that most Westerners believe that even though some people become rich by acting badly, they still enjoy a luxurious and happy life. Buddhists do not think that this is possible. Bad actions will catch up with a person sooner or later. I strongly believe that businesspeople who earn their wealth honestly and share some of it with others will be happier than those who cheat or behave like the one-eyed man.

The Proper Use of Wealth

Buddha also presented eight questions that leaders and businesspeople can ask themselves if they want to know if they are using their wealth in proper ways. Though they may seem obvious to some, the "best" answers are indicated in brackets after each question.

- Did you acquire wealth lawfully? (Yes, I did.)
- Did your wealth provide happiness only to you? (No, also to others.)
- Did your wealth provide happiness also to others? (Yes, it did.)
- Did you share your wealth with others? (Yes, I did.)
- Did you carry out any good deeds with your wealth? (Yes, I did.)
- Are you attached to and infatuated with your wealth? (No, I am not.)

People too "attached to" their wealth are those who have become stingy and greedy. Those who are "infatuated" think they are very important, deserve to be respected, and know the right answer to every question, simply because they are wealthy.

- Are you heedful of the dangers of wealth? (Yes, I am.)

"Heedfulness" is an important concept in Buddhism. Similar to mindfulness, it means being aware of what is going on in one's mind. A heedful leader will recognize when his or her mind becomes infatuated or stingy with his or her wealth and will stop the process in its tracks.

- Do you possess the insight that leads to spiritual freedom? (Yes, I do.)

"Insight that leads to spiritual freedom" refers to an understanding that wealth can increase and decrease for reasons a person cannot control. There is nothing wrong with being happy when wealth increases, but it is wrong to become unhappy when it decreases. If someone becomes overly attached to his wealth, he loses his spiritual freedom and becomes worried about anything that would reduce his wealth.

Businesspeople can grade themselves using this list. The highest level is reached by those who seek wealth lawfully and in so doing provide happiness for themselves and others. They share their wealth and perform good deeds; moreover, they are not attached to or infatuated with their wealth, they are heedful of its dangers, and they possess the insight that leads to spiritual freedom.

However, contrary to what some may believe, Buddha never praised or advocated poverty. He thought at an early stage in his life that he could become happy by living in a forest and starving himself close to death. He found that this did not work and concluded that it was not the right way. That is why he recommended that monks and nuns lead a modest but comfortable life. He saw poverty as the cause of immorality and crime and suggested that in order to eradicate crime, people's economic condition should be improved. That is why he believed grain (for sowing) and other facilities for agriculture should be provided to farmers and cultivators and that, in a crisis, capital should be provided for traders and businesspeople. He strongly believed that adequate wages should be paid to those who are employed. When people are provided for and are earning sufficient income, they will be content and will have no fear or anxiety, and consequently the country will be peaceful and free from crime.[5]

A Living Entity

Organizational-development specialist Peter Senge points out another reason why looking at a business as simply a moneymaking machine is erroneous: a machine wears out, whereas a business can renew itself; it may become obsolete, but that is because of poor performance by its employees or because of market conditions.[6] A machine cannot be motivated; it does what it is programmed to do. Members of an organization, however, do need to be motivated to realize the purpose of the business. Furthermore, a machine is not conscious and does not have a conscience, whereas an organization can be seen to have a shared consciousness and a shared conscience. It is thus much more appropriate to look at a business as a living entity than as a machine.

Organizational-learning consultant Arie de Geus expands on this:

> *All companies exhibit the behaviour and certain characteristics of living entities. All companies learn. All companies, whether explicitly or not, have an identity that determines their coherence. All companies build relationships with other entities, and all companies grow and develop until they die. . . . Like all organisms, the living company exists primarily for its own survival and improvement: to fulfill its potential and to become as great as it can be.[7]*

It is interesting to think of a business as having a conscience, in the sense of knowing what is right and wrong. If the sense of what is right and wrong varies enormously among individuals, it is even more complicated for businesses. A company's conscience incorporates those of many people with different ideas of what is right and wrong. Yet because this conscience is collective, it is easy to diffuse responsibility or deflect blame when a wrong decision is made. In fact, research shows that people in business will do things they would not do in their private lives. That proves that the actions of a business as a whole influence the conscience of individuals within it. This influence can make people act better or worse than they would on their own. Unfortunately, the influence of business on the moral standards of the individual can be negative, especially when business leaders put pressure on employees to produce profits, without emphasizing the overriding importance of those profits being gained honestly based on Right Conduct and Right View. This is why, as a business leader, infusing your company with an ethical purpose and a strong set of values is so important.

A human being has a physical body that includes a brain, a consciousness, and a conscience. A business is not such an integrated system. Offices, equipment, machines, inventories, shops, computers, and so on are not like a body. They have no sensors that communicate with the brain. These physical things are only of value in their relationship to the people who use them, and then only as those people relate to one another in a network among the employees, their customers, and suppliers.

Nevertheless, this difference is not as large as you may think. What is a person without a network of relationships with family, friends, and acquaintances? A person truly "exists" only through relationships with others. Likewise, a business consists of an invisible network of relations among people. The true value of a business is not the sum of its facilities and its employees and its financial resources: the value resides in the relationships among the people within it and with the many stakeholders outside it.

Business and Happiness

Businesses are not normally thought of as producers of happiness. When I started on this project, I was not sure to what extent businesses would be able and willing to see creating happiness as one of their goals. But I now see that is a real possibility.

I believe that the desire to be happy and avoid suffering is universal. At the superficial level, different cultures have different ideas and norms about what constitutes happiness. But there are certain notions of happiness on which people universally agree. Nobody wants to be poor, lacking shelter, sufficient food, or the means to send their children to school. No one wants to be without friends, be disrespected by others, or not have the freedom to express an opinion. As the United Nations Universal Declaration of Human Rights states, "Everyone has the right to life, liberty and security of person" and "All human beings are born free and equal in dignity and rights."[8] But once these basic needs are met, most people in most cultures would also define happiness as being intellectually, emotionally, and spiritually fulfilled in their lives. As Laurens explains, satisfaction in one's work and career can play a large role in this. Which is why, despite what some may think, business leaders are responsible to a large degree for the basic happiness of their employees.

Psychologist Abraham Maslow developed the concept that happiness depended on satisfying different needs and that some fundamental needs had to be satisfied before others could be considered.[9] This is referred to as the "hierarchy of needs" and is often presented as a pyramid with five levels.

Maslow claimed that people had to satisfy the basic needs of food, water, and shelter before moving up to the next level. Naturally, income is necessary to satisfy these needs. People at low levels of income may be able to focus only on the basic needs and thus are often satisfied with almost any job that provides food, water, shelter, et cetera. But when those needs are satisfied, people are no longer happy with just any job: they want an interesting job that contributes to their higher-level needs, like self-respect, independence, freedom, and, eventually, "self-actualization." People can reach that stage only if they feel that all their talents and capabilities are being used to their fullest potential.

Having a job plays a role in achieving all levels of needs. It provides income to buy food and shelter (level 1) and to achieve safety and stability (level 2). A company is a kind of community with personal relationships; most people establish friendships with some of their colleagues at work, and at the very least want to feel a sense of belonging in the workplace (level 3). A job can also give self-respect and independence (level 4), and, for those lucky enough to be in a job that allows them to be all they can be, can even foster self-actualization (level 5). This should be the goal for business leaders: to create a culture in which their employees can achieve the highest level of needs.

Workers find greater meaning in their work, their organizations, and their lives when their role within the organization in achieving its purpose is recognized—better yet, celebrated—on a regular basis.

Leaders have an enormous influence on the well-being of their employees beyond providing a job and paying a salary. Many employee-satisfaction studies conclude that "trust" is one of the most important factors. Employees want to feel that they are trusted by management and that they can trust management in return. People also want to feel they have enough freedom to perform a good job. If they have no freedom and everything they do is inspected and micromanaged, employees quickly become unhappy. They perceive this not only as a lack of trust, but also as a lack of respect.

One way for leaders to show respect for their people is by investing in training and development. People who are constantly being challenged and given opportunities to learn new skills are far more likely to achieve a sense of self-actualization. People should also be informed of how the business is doing and what the future looks like; honest communication breeds respect and self-esteem— level 4 needs. In other words, jobs provide income and income provides freedom: freedom to pay for shelter, food, health care, and education. But jobs also provide self-respect and the possibility to grow materially and spiritually. A company that does this can create significant happiness.

Maslow's theory reminds me of a story from the Buddhist tradition. Buddha arranged a meeting with a peasant named Alavi to give him some teaching. Buddha walked for miles and was warmly welcomed by the inhabitants of the town where the peasant lived, but Alavi himself was not there; he was off chasing one of his cows that had escaped. When the peasant returned, he was exhausted and very hungry. When Buddha saw Alavi's condition, he asked the city elders to arrange some food for the poor man; only when the peasant had eaten his fill and was refreshed did the Buddha start to teach. The Buddha afterward explained his reasons: "When people are overwhelmed and in pain through suffering, they are incapable of understanding religious teaching."[10]

In other words, level 1 needs, the physiological needs for food and rest, first have to be satisfied before the higher levels—such as mental and spiritual enlightenment—can be activated.

Happiness in the Maslow model is based on the assumption that the needs at all five levels can be satisfied. In contrast, according to the Buddhist way of thinking, it is impossible ever to satisfy all these needs. To a Buddhist, the objective is also happiness, but in the sense of "peace of mind," not of "satisfying all needs." By training the mind to avoid thoughts and actions that lead to suffering, and also to cope with adverse events that will inevitably happen, such as old age, loss of family members, or loss of wealth, happiness or "acceptance" can be achieved.

The basis of Maslow's theory is to satisfy the needs of the individual, of the self. According to Buddhist thinking, in contrast, there is no independent, permanent, unchanging self. The self consists of relationships with other people and other aspects of the physical environment. All people, not least in Western society, are obsessed by the "self": "This is mine," "I am being offended," "I do not make enough money," or "People are not nice to me." In the Buddhist concept, it is not other people who have to satisfy the needs of an individual; it is the reverse. People can be happy only if they satisfy the needs of other people as well as their own.

Money Can't Buy Happiness

A wealth of data in recent decades has shown that once the needs of food, shelter, and basic comfort have been met, increased wealth has little bearing on happiness. In other words, "money can't buy happiness." However, many people in industrialized nations fail to realize this, and so they seek more and more wealth, rather than a greater sense of belonging or activities that lead them toward self-actualization. And so happiness eludes them. They are obsessed with wealth and focus on unwholesome rather than wholesome consumption. Remember that unwholesome consumption uses goods and services merely to satisfy desires and for ego gratification, while wholesome consumption contributes to the well-being of others.

One factor that contributes to this obsession with wealth in many industrialized countries is a phenomenon known as "keeping up with the Joneses." People often strive to maintain the same—or a higher—standard of living as their peers. If a neighbor switches to a flat-panel television, they want to do the same. If they cannot afford this, it produces unhappiness. Equally, though, if they can afford it, they run up against economist Fred Hirsch's concept of "positional goods," which have a value in relation to their high status or scarcity. If everyone had a Ferrari, for example, it would no longer hold the same cachet as a possession. Happiness in this consumer context is therefore never attainable.[11]

There is an increasing amount of research into what happiness is and how it can be measured. Ranging from those by economists such as Richard Layard and Andrew Oswald to those by psychologists such as Ed Diener and Martin Seligman,[12] more than 1,700 studies have been conducted on happiness and wealth in over forty countries.[13] Many of these have shown that, as Buddhism teaches, wealth and happiness are not positively correlated.

Professor Ruut Veenhoven at Erasmus University, who maintains the World Database of Happiness,[14] for example, found that when people are poor, their happiness on average rises with their income. But if income is above a certain level, happiness stays constant. One's income level is important, but the direction of change is significant too. When income is increasing, people are obviously much happier than when it is declining. Someone with a higher income that is declining is less happy than someone with a lower income that is increasing.

Nevertheless, money is not the only factor. Bruno Frey and Alois Stutzer, two prominent Swiss economists, concluded, not surprisingly, that having a job makes an important contribution to happiness but that genetic makeup is also relevant: Extroverts are happier than introverts. Family life and friends are important too, as are good health and one's position relative to one's peers.[15]

Buddhists believe that people's dispositions differ and—this is very important—that regardless of their disposition at birth, everyone can improve the way they are. For example, someone who is a pessimist can strengthen his self-confidence through training the mind, which in turn increases his happiness. Buddha said, "Self-confidence is the greatest treasure man can have." He also said, "The master should assign tasks to the workmen in accordance to their abilities."[16]

This is an area where a company can make an important contribution. When people succeed in reaching the goals they or others want them to meet, self-confidence grows. Companies working in this way will increase the self-confidence of their employees and as a consequence the employees' happiness. In this way, pessimism is reduced and optimism increased. This is exactly why His Holiness teaches that the role of businesses should not be to simply earn money or create wealth—but to foster true happiness.

What Organizations Can Do to Create True Happiness

Organizations have the capacity to create job satisfaction and even go beyond that to foster general happiness among their people. What can an organization do, in terms of policies and values, to spread that happiness? Here is a short list of ideas:

- *Conduct satisfaction surveys of employees to gauge how people are feeling about the organization's policies and procedures, and especially about the way management behaves. Take corrective action based on the results to raise morale and job satisfaction (one element of happiness).*

- *Allow and encourage flexible and diverse work schedules for employees so they have more time to devote to their families and other interests. Luckily, new technologies and new ways of working have made this increasingly possible.*

- *Invest in training and personal development programs for employees. This conveys a message of both respect and trust, contributing to an employee's sense of satisfaction and encouraging self-actualization.*

- *Make sure that employees understand how they are contributing to the success of the organization, at whatever level they work. Also make sure that they feel the company is aware of and appreciates their contribution.*

- *Commit to wealth creation for all employees, including reviewing pay policies and structures, doing away with unnecessary imbalances, and rewarding all contributors to success.*

- *Create corporate responsibility statements for company employees to abide by. These can include environmental policies that address overconsumption or waste of material goods. "Export" such policies to all overseas partners and subsidiaries to promote equity and wealth creation in new markets. (There is more on corporate responsibility in chapter 6.)*

- *Engage in responsible advertising of products and services that does not promote a purely consumption-based economy; appeal to the higher-level needs of the consumer. Avoid promoting unwholesome consumption.*
- *Consider any downsizing plans carefully. Loss of jobs, and therefore income, can lead to widespread unhappiness. Take all available steps to prevent such an occurrence, or, at the very least, assist employees in finding new jobs. Keep their collective well-being in mind.*
- *Lead by example. As a leader, take the opportunity to show satisfaction with life by exhibiting a trained mind and balanced lifestyle.*

And, as we shall see in part 3, there are also many opportunities for businesses and organizations to foster happiness not just among their employees but on a global scale. As we will see, organizations can help solve some of the problems of poverty, injustice, and environmental sustainability throughout the world.

We often say in Buddhism that people should free themselves of wants. By "wants" we mean insatiable desires. Buddha said, "You should be satisfied with what you have but never be satisfied with the amount of good you have carried out." In the Buddhist tradition, genuine happiness can be achieved only by people who act perfectly virtuously, who have no negative thoughts and emotions.

Of course, Buddhists recognize that acquiring wealth is one of life's fundamental activities. Consumption and wealth acquisition are natural, but if done the wrong way, they can lead to suffering. Someone who consumes for the sake of consuming, without any restraints, will not be happy. Buddha recommended that in prosperous periods part of one's gains should be set aside to deal with lean periods. If wealth is earned dishonestly, it means it has been stolen from others or earned in a way that causes other forms of harm. If wealth is not used to benefit other people, it will not provide any happiness for the owner or anybody else. In order for it to lead to happiness, wealth has to be earned honestly and put to good use.

I have listened to and participated in endless discussions on whether profit should be the only purpose of business. For me, the answer is simple. Profits are a condition for survival, but their *purpose* is to make a contribution to the well-being of society at large.

6

Doing Business Right

In Buddhism we believe that the reputation of a company depends on whether it operates with a warm and strong heart. A person who has a warm heart, someone who follows Right Conduct, is actively concerned with the well-being of others. And good actions are as important for a company as they are for a person, perhaps even more so, since, as we have seen, so many people are affected by the actions of a company.

As we saw in chapter 2, humility is one of the character traits of a good leader. Flashy, egocentric executives are more likely to put their own interests and pleasures over acting as good citizens. When leaders show tendencies to bad or unwholesome actions, such as dishonesty, they put their organizations at risk. The consequences of a poor reputation are often hard to overcome.

When I read about corporate scandals, the main cause always appears to be a craving for power, wealth, or fame by the company's leaders. This craving leads to dishonesty and law breaking. If you think back to the basic principles of Buddhism that we discussed earlier, there are warnings about the suffering that comes about from uncontrolled desire or craving. The leaders involved in these scandals have untrained minds and have become victims of their own negative tendencies and unwholesome emotions. I consider this a great shame, as many of these leaders no doubt have talent and hold the potential to do good in the world.

But the blame doesn't rest solely on the shoulders of these leaders. In a sense, the system is to blame as well. Take the example of pay disparity. I find it very disturbing that the heads of companies earn many millions of dollars while some of their employees receive salaries that don't allow them a decent standard of living. I accept that people with great artistic, physical, or entrepreneurial talent can become wealthy, but that wealth need not come at the expense of others. The only way to truly solve this problem is for leaders to exercise self-restraint and, again, to consider the well-being of everyone in their decision making.

Some organizations—oil companies, for instance—face difficult ethical dilemmas that make it hard for them to balance the needs of their employees with the greater good of society. It is unrealistic to expect these companies to limit their activities to countries with good governance. They will have to cope with weak, unstable, or corrupt governments. They may have to make decisions that may harm the environment. However, they should make extra effort to make the best of a difficult situation and wield their power responsibly and ethically.

Given their wide reach and influence, global companies should always strive to operate at the very highest level of integrity. And it is not enough that they simply act ethically themselves; they should choose partners and suppliers that operate at a high level of responsibility. This will reward those organizations that have the best interests of society at heart.

Doing What Is Right

Being seen as a company with high ethical standards not only is taking Right Conduct; it also has enormous business value, in tangible and measurable ways. Such a company finds it much easier to attract and keep top-class employees. If clients or customers have a positive opinion of a company, they are likely to continue buying from it. Furthermore, loyal customers not only continue to buy but promote the company by word of mouth and other means, thereby contributing to its sustained profitability and growth. A company with an image of high quality and good service can charge a higher price for its products, as studies have shown that people are willing to pay a premium for products from socially responsible companies. People are also more willing to try a new product from a company they trust than from an unknown company or from a company with a questionable reputation. Additionally, the share price of a company with a good reputation tends to be higher than that of one with the same financial performance and a poor reputation. Such a company can borrow funds at a lower rate of interest. And employees' pride in an organization is all the greater if it is perceived to be ethical, assuring greater employee engagement and motivation—which in turn drives profit. The list goes on.

In short, a good reputation is the most important asset that a global company can have. Yet it has become much more difficult to develop and maintain in recent times because of the rising expectations of the public, the critical media, and the oversight of many watchdogs; companies are vulnerable at every turn. Nothing can destroy the value of a company more quickly than the public exposure of grossly dishonest behavior by its top management— which is why it is that much more important for companies today to act in accordance with the Buddhist principles of Right View and Right Conduct.

The Causes of Public Mistrust

If you ask people their feelings on big business and its leaders, chances are they will respond with some negative or cynical impressions of the "corporate machine." Recent business scandals have led to a widespread distrust of business in general.

So leaders should be alert to several practices that are particularly alarming to the public; if detected within an organization, they should be addressed and rectified as soon as possible.

Creative or Fraudulent Accounting

There have been a number of recent examples of companies falsifying accounts, knowingly giving false financial information to the public, or engaging in price fixing or insider trading. Such scandals occur all over the world: think of ABB, Ahold, Christie's, Daewoo, Enron, Hoffmann–La Roche, Hollinger International, Parmalat, Sotheby's; the list goes on. In almost all instances, high-level executives are directly involved, which underscores the need for the type of leader we describe in this book. Even though the punishment can be quite severe, involving huge fines and prison sentences, it is unrealistic to expect that these scandals will totally disappear, as the pressure for CEOs to provide increasing profits is paramount. Until the role of the organization is reframed as something greater than maximizing shareholder value, the risk of fraud will remain. It is important to remember, however, that only a small percentage of all companies engage in this kind of practice.

Increasing Disparity in Compensation

Many people think it is unfair that the compensation of top managers is increasing much more rapidly than that of other employees, especially those with what is already the lowest pay. People largely accept that successful entrepreneurs, entertainers, or athletes can make inordinate sums of money but consider it immoral when the compensation of professional managers keeps rising much faster than that of other employees. For example, the average compensation package of the top CEOs in the United States has increased from $480,000 to $8 million in *the last twenty-five years, while the average worker's pay is now $27,000, a figure that over the same period has hardly kept up with inflation.[1]*

Companies have been unable to convince people that they are acting fairly in this matter. One of the reasons executive pay has risen so dramatically is that having a competent and inspiring CEO is fundamental for a company to be successful, yet such people are not easy to find. Those who are able to turn around a declining company, like Carlos Ghosn at Nissan or Lou Gerstner at IBM, are "stars"—just like popular actors or starting quarterbacks—and as such can command astonishing compensation packages. It is important to remember, though, that these stars are only a very small percentage of the total number of overpaid CEOs. If companies and boards could exert more control over compensation and tie it more closely to performance, such businesses would likely see highly improved morale and therefore better results in the end. At American Express, for example, chief executive Ken Chenault's pay package now includes an option on 2.75 million shares. However, he will receive the full grant of shares only if AmEx's performance reaches some very high targets over a long horizon—for example, an increase in revenue by at least 10 percent a year over the next six years. Tying executive compensation more closely to performance in this manner is an approach for other companies to consider.[2]

Exploitative Practices

Unfortunately, exploitative practices are exceedingly common in industries that depend on rare natural resources, such as oil and mining. Ironically, several of the largest oil and gas companies, such as Royal Dutch/Shell and BP, are among the most active in implementing the principles of social responsibility and corporate citizenship (an area we shall consider in more depth later in this chapter). But such companies have also made several widely publicized "errors," particularly in the area of environmental violations. For example, BP created headlines with a large oil spill in Alaska, and Shell was involved in the now-famous Brent Spar debacle, which we will discuss in the next section.

Unfortunately, the very nature of mineral, gas, and oil exploration and production is exploitative, which makes it difficult to maintain ethical practices. Minerals and oil reserves are found in several poor countries, but often they cannot be sold inside the countries concerned and have to be exported. So the potential benefits that the natural resources might contribute to the country may be "stolen" by an economic elite—by, or in cooperation with, the government. Instead of being a blessing for a country, such resources often turn out to be a curse.

That said, there are positive steps that these companies can take. Many oil companies, when starting a new project, conduct an environmental- and social-impact study before reaching a decision to proceed. Lately, some companies have included in these studies representatives of the communities that will be affected by the project. Large companies are also investing significant R & D effort in the area of renewable energy. It is the task of making the public aware of those efforts that remains difficult.

Marketing of Harmful Products

In chapter 2, we talked about the Buddhist principle of Right Livelihood, a component of which urges companies against engaging in the production of harmful products. Many products that are harmful to the public's well-being are legal, and even very profitable, yet companies in those industries risk negative publicity and backlash from concerned consumer and public-interest groups.

Consider the tobacco giant Philip Morris, which, thanks to many lawsuits and other PR problems, is still trying to dig itself out of the hole. Add to that the fact that smoking has become an unpopular and virtually taboo activity in many countries and Philip Morris finds itself needing to re-create its image yet again. Public opinion is very powerful, and companies that promote or produce harmful products will, in the end, suffer damage to their reputation.

Human Rights and Environmental Violations

In this age of globalization, many international organizations are being taken to task on their labor practices in developing and poor countries. Watchdog groups are continually alert for both human rights and environmental violations. Companies must be willing to make clear their policies in both areas and apply them to all agreements and contracts with both official partners and unofficial vendors. Otherwise, they run the risk of being associated with practices that ultimately will cost them their reputation.

The Credible Corporation

Today, being seen by the public as credible and ethical is one of the biggest competitive advantages a company can have. More than ever before, the challenge for a business leader is to win back the favor of the public and to change people's expectations of what business can contribute. We are not talking about PR or "spin" here, but about what a company actually does. Below we describe a couple of ways to help organizations better establish their credibility in accordance with the principles of Right View and Right Conduct.

Promote Corporate Citizenship

Corporate citizenship, as we saw in chapter 4, is the idea that a company must act as a responsible member of society, just as an individual citizen should. The strength of a company's commitment to corporate citizenship is becoming an issue of increasing importance to shareholders, as companies are now being ranked on indexes such as the Dow Jones Sustainability World Index,

Dow Jones STOXX, FTSE4Good Global 100, and the FTSE4Good Europe 50. To be included in these indexes, companies have to prove that they act in accordance with principles of social responsibility. Consider the following statistics:

- *Over two hundred companies globally have responded to more stringent environmental criteria to improve their practices, with eighty-five being deleted from these indexes for not doing enough to meet the challenge.*
- *Fifty-eight companies have moved to meet the new, tougher human rights criteria, with only twenty being deleted.*
- *Twenty companies to date have improved their policies, management systems, and reporting on supply-chain labor standards, with two being deleted.[3]*

In other words, companies are now under increasing pressure to reach new levels of corporate citizenship. On an international level, the Organisation for Economic Co-operation and Development (OECD) has published guidelines offering "recommendations to international business for conduct in such areas as labour, environment, consumer protection and the fight against corruption"[4] and the United Nations has established the Global Compact, described as "the world's largest, global corporate citizenship initiative."[5] According to a survey published in the World Bank Report 2005, 20 percent of companies indicate that the OECD guidelines have influenced their business, and that figure is around 30 percent for the Global Compact. Organizations that are able to demonstrate their adherence to such principles not only provide benefits to society at large but also gain a substantial boost to their credibility.

Nevertheless, adherence to such guidelines should be reflected in the actions of the company, rather than merely in its PR. A survey by McKinsey reported some interesting statistics:

- More than 90 percent of CEOs are doing more than they did five years ago to incorporate environmental, social, and governance issues into strategy and operations.
- 72 percent of CEOs said that companies should fully embed corporate responsibility into strategy and operations, but only 50 percent think their firms actually do so.
- 59 percent of CEOs said corporate responsibility should be embedded into global supply chains, but only 27 percent of CEOs think they are doing so.[6]

As a leader, it is your responsibility to ensure that your company meets its stated commitment to corporate citizenship.

Accept That Honesty and Success Can Coexist

Many businesspeople claim that business is a fight to the death and take a "no-holds-barred" approach to competition. With this attitude and approach, there is not much room for honesty or integrity. Naturally, this kind of talk gives business a poor image. But the conversation can be changed. Honesty and business success can coexist.

More and more, companies are seeking to operate in an ethical manner and be recognized for their actions. Ethisphere magazine recently selected one hundred of the "world's most ethical companies" from thousands of candidates. As Alex Brigham, the magazine's executive editor, explained:

> *We looked for absolutes. We examined companies in relational context of their industries. And we looked for influential leadership that moved others to change or follow. Companies were measured in a rigorous eight-step process and then scored against nine distinct ethical leadership criteria. . . . These organizations go beyond making statements about doing business ethically; they translate those words into action.[7]*

One organization on the list is Fluor, a Texas-based Fortune 500 company that provides engineering and procurement services, largely to the U.S. government. As the reputation of one of its competitors, Halliburton, has become tarnished with claims of corruption and cronyism, Fluor's is on the rise. Alan Boeckmann, Fluor Corporation's chairman and CEO, explains that "ethics and ethical behavior are core values at Fluor and have been since our inception more than a century ago."[8] And the company has the profits to show for it.

Sandy Cutler, CEO of Eaton Corporation, a diversified industrial manufacturer that is also on the Ethisphere list, believes that ethics is not merely a compliance issue. Rather, "it's about doing business right through internal

philosophies and customer commitments. We'll lose
business before we will compromise our values." He adds
that if a company is committed to doing business ethically,
"you can cut the top off and the bottom would keep
working."[9]

Aiming for Virtue at GE

The world has changed. Businesses today aren't
admired. . . . There's a bigger gulf today between
haves and have-nots than ever before. It's up to us
to use our platform to be good citizens, because not
only is it a nice thing to do, it's a business impera-
tive. Good leaders give back. The era in which we
live belongs to people who believe in themselves,
but are focused on the needs of others.[10]

Jeff Immelt, Chief Executive, GE

General Electric (GE) is one of the world's most prominent
companies, with 320,000 employees, about half of whom
work outside the United States, and a market capitali-
zation of $375 billion at the end of 2007. Its chief
executive until 2000, Jack Welch, was considered one of the
most visionary managers of our time. Many people doubted
that his successor, Jeff Immelt, would be able to maintain
the same high level of performance. To the pleasant
surprise of GE shareholders, Immelt was in fact highly
successful—due in no small part to his commitment to
"corporate citizenship" upon assuming the post of CEO.

*Immelt told the two hundred members of top management
that it would take "virtue" to keep the company on top.*

*Why did Immelt add the goal of attaining virtue? One
reason was to improve GE's reputation; he knew that
nothing can reduce the value of a company as fast as a
reputational problem. Recall how Arthur Andersen, an
accounting firm with seventy thousand employees, virtually
closed up shop overnight after its reputation became
tarnished in connection with the Enron scandal in
the United States, or how 40 percent of the market
capitalization ($9 billion of the market value) of Marsh &
McLennan, a large insurance and financial institution,
disappeared when it was accused of making profits
dishonestly.*

*He also knew that an increasing number of institutional
investors are demanding to know if a company is acting
responsibly in all aspects of its operations—in other words,
that virtue makes for a more marketable stock.*

*Another reason Immelt placed such importance on the
company's virtue was to motivate GE's employees. He
knew that employees prefer working for a company that,
as Immelt says, "makes a difference, a company that is
doing great things in the world."*

*Perhaps the most important reason is GE's ambition
to be excellent in all it does. Every year, the company
organizes a three-week program for executives in their
thirties and forties who are expected to become GE leaders
in the future, taking up different themes each time. In
2002, Immelt asked the group to study corporate social
responsibility. Its members asked a large number of*

prominent companies, investors, regulators, and activists about GE's reputation in relation to social responsibility. The result was very negative: GE ranked quite low compared to other large companies.

And Immelt's commitment to virtue was more than just empty words. Under his leadership, GE instituted a training program to make all employees aware of the importance of virtue. Management started a crash course to improve environmental performance in the company's own activities and acquired a maker of solar-energy equipment, a water-purification company, and a wind-energy business partner. GE performed audits of its suppliers in the developing world to make sure they complied with environmental, health, and labor standards. As a result, it decided not do business in Myanmar (Burma), because the government was a notorious human-rights violator. GE started dialogues with socially responsible investment funds and in 2004 was admitted to the Dow Jones Sustainability Index and became one of three hundred best-in-class companies.

Immelt understood the Buddhist principle of impermanence and knew that if the company did not adapt to the growing public concern over social responsibility, it would not survive. As someone with a trained mind who acted with humility rather than conceit and arrogance, he knew he could not make these complex changes alone. He therefore appointed a vice president for corporate citizenship to help drive positive change in the organization.

GE is also a strong believer in the merit of diversity among its employees. The company won high-profile *awards for promoting women and African Americans into its executive ranks. People in GE's African American Forum asked Immelt whether the company could do more in Africa. Although he could not identify a business to be located on that continent, he did decide to invest $20 million in a health-care project in Ghana, a country in which GE does almost no business. He said that he could justify such a project without any return on investment in several ways:*

- *If you look at the long term, there is a decent chance that the continent of Africa will become a market that we want to understand.*
- *For young African Americans, there's an incredible fascination with Africa. They view this as extremely positive.*
- *We do this project because GE wants to be known as a good company, not just in the United States but around the world.*

"Virtue" refers to moral excellence. Under Immelt, GE has proven itself to be a company that acts with virtue, or what Buddhists refer to as Right Conduct. I am convinced that if many other businesses did the same, they would not only make a positive difference in the world, but would also see measurable business results.

GE is not just making pious statements or angling for positive PR. It has taken action by putting somebody in charge who is committed to virtue and who has put actual efforts and resources behind this commitment. This shows that GE's leadership is effectively using the principles of Right View and Right Conduct.

"Gulliver and Lilliput" at Shell

The Brent Spar was a 167-meter-tall (almost twice as high as Big Ben) oil storage buoy owned by the Shell Oil Company. With its tanks empty, it weighed about 14,500 tons, roughly as much as a large cruise ship. Once Shell no longer needed the buoy, it obtained approval from the British government to sink it in the North Atlantic. Yet despite the multinational's economic and political clout, protests by the environmental organization Greenpeace and the subsequent negative media coverage forced it to abandon this plan.

Heinz Rothermund (managing director of Shell UK Exploration) commented:

> *Brent Spar has transformed our outlook. Spar is not as many believe an environmental problem, rather it will go down in history as a symbol of the industry's inability to engage with the outside world.[11]*

Rothermund recognized that Shell had failed to consider the effect of its actions on the public at large. A leader with an untrained mind might have responded differently—perhaps with anger toward Greenpeace for staging such public protests and thwarting Shell's plans for the buoy—but instead, Rothermund avoided negative emotions and opted to learn from the incident. He concluded that the company, in the future, needed to be more concerned about the reaction of society at large to its actions. It also had to accept that many people would not trust the statements it made about its environmental performance: it is not a question of "tell me" but "prove it to me."

Cor Herkströter, then chairman of Shell's Committee of Managing Directors, made the following commitment:

> *We hope by our future actions to show that the basic interests of business and society are entirely compatible—that there does not have to be a choice between profits and principles.[12]*

Shell was among the first companies to put the principles of ethical behavior into a document and to encourage employees to apply them.

Another consequence of the Brent Spar incident was that Shell embraced the principle of "engagement," meaning involving the input of different organizations outside the company in its decision-making process. These external organizations do not have formal authority over the decisions that Shell eventually makes, but they do have an important informal influence because Shell listens carefully to their opinions, explains its own views in return, and engages in a constructive dialogue.

In an article written ten years after the Brent Spar debacle, country chairman of Shell UK James Smith wrote:

> *We had learned that, while good science and regulatory approval are essential, they are not sufficient. We needed to engage with society—understanding and responding to people's concerns and expectations. . . . We have to consult as early and fully as*

possible and be willing to listen and change. We must admit mistakes and demonstrate both that we try to put things right and to learn.[13]

That, indeed, is Right Conduct.

The Role of NGOs

As can be seen from the Brent Spar example, nongovernmental organizations (NGOs) and the media have a great deal of influence on a company's reputation. Without the actions of Greenpeace, the Brent Spar incident would never have hit the headlines. Not only did this NGO end up wielding more power than Shell, but it even forced the governments of the UK and Germany to reverse their decisions (no small feat, given the company's backing by powerful shareholders, even more powerful lobbyists, and the UK government). As Chris Fay, chief executive of Shell UK, wrote:

> *Shell UK had been ordered by its parent company, the Royal Dutch Shell group, to abandon deep-sea disposal, because other European subsidiaries were finding themselves in an untenable position. . . . The Shell Group has had to react to its failure to persuade ministers in certain European governments to adhere to treaties they are party to.*[14]

Most NGOs see their responsibility as looking after the public good, not the good of business. By and large, they concern themselves with large global companies, less so with small- to medium-sized businesses. And their actions have a great influence on how the public views the companies they hold under the microscope. Unfortunately for companies, the credibility of NGOs with the public at large is considerably higher than that of global businesses.

Most NGO employees are intellectually bright and good communicators with strong moral convictions. Given these characteristics and the sometimes substantial size and geographical spread of NGOs, they are important actors in the global economy. Most large companies are taking a constructive approach to them, although this does not mean that they will do whatever NGOs think is best. It means that they engage NGOs in constructive dialogue and in some cases give contracts to NGOs to undertake studies for them. For example, telecommunications company BT contracted an NGO to study the consequences of outsourcing some of its UK activities to India. When sports apparel marketer Nike found that its inspectors were not able to uncover unacceptable treatment of workers among its suppliers, it engaged an NGO, which found the problem quickly. The employees did not trust the company inspectors but did trust the NGO.

As was true in the Shell case, NGOs and the media reinforce each other. NGOs are skillful in mobilizing media interest, and together they have a very strong influence on the reputations of companies, making it essential for businesses to understand how they operate.

The growth and influence of NGOs form an interesting phenomenon. I must admit to having a bias for organizations that are looking after the public good, but I do have a concern that NGOs do not take a holistic view, that they are narrowing in on a particular cause most of the time. It is unreasonable to ask them to understand business better than the leaders themselves. However, if by questioning actions the importance of Right View and Right Conduct is highlighted, this benefits everyone.

In the Shell case, it appears the company lacked humility. Its managers thought, "We know best, we've studied the alternative disposal methods, we've received the approval of the government of the UK. What more could one ask?" This worked against them. The question Shell should have asked was: "How will people react when they find out that we are sinking a large, dirty steel structure in the sea?" If the leaders at Shell had understood the Buddhist principle of interdependence, they would have recognized the negative impact of Shell's actions on the opinion of people at large and might have anticipated Greenpeace's response.

In this case, the government leaders, too, lost contact with reality—and, again, by "reality" I mean seeing things the way they really are. Neither the governments nor the company had foreseen the strong feelings that a large number of people had about the "holiness" of the sea. Emotional reactions are a part of reality. If strong emotions are involved, they should be dealt with constructively. In this case, people became angry, and significant effort was required to deal with that anger. From that point of view, I am sure that the idea of "engagement" is the right course for today's businesses. Engagement means taking a considered view of the situation and analyzing all outcomes before choosing the course of action that puts the well-being of society before the well-being of the company or the individual leader.

The challenge for business is to explain to the public that "good" companies do exist. Organizations should band together in that effort. If leaders lay out their principles and then act authentically, the reputation of businesses will improve, and one of the benefits will be more loyal customers.

When I started this project, I was not sure that companies could act in such a way that they could deserve a thoroughly good reputation. Now I am convinced that they can. And I consider this goal very important for individual organizations and for society as a whole.

Creating positive change for all is among the most challenging and yet rewarding of all tasks for a leader. But remember, if you as a leader run your life—and your company—with virtue and a warm heart, greater happiness, satisfaction—and profit—will result.

Part 3

[Leading in an Interconnected World]

Leadership that acknowledges universal

responsibility is the real key to overcoming

the world's problems.

7

The Challenge of Globalization

The world is becoming increasingly interdependent, and that is why I firmly believe in the need to develop a sense of universal responsibility. We need to think in global terms, because the effects of one nation's actions are felt far beyond its borders. The acceptance of universally binding standards of human rights is essential in today's shrinking world. Respect for fundamental human rights should not be an ideal but a requisite foundation for every human society.

Artificial barriers dividing nations and peoples have fallen in recent times. The success of the popular people's movements in dismantling the East-West division, which had polarized the whole world for decades, has been a source of great hope and expectations. Yet there still remains a major gulf at the heart of the human family. If we are serious in our commitment to the fundamental principles of equality—principles that, I believe, lie at the heart of the concept of human rights—today's economic disparities can no longer be ignored. It is not enough merely to state that all human beings must enjoy equal dignity. This must be translated into action. We have a responsibility to find ways to achieve a more equitable distribution of the world's resources.[1]

I am, in principle, in favor of "globalization" and the concept of "global" companies. In the past, communities and countries could live in isolation if they wanted to; that is no longer the case. Today, a stock-market crash on one side of the globe has a direct and immediate effect on the other side. Terrorism born in one country can destabilize a dozen others. And the effects of poverty, disease, and social unrest in a handful of nations impact the rest of the world. It is my opinion that global companies can be agents for positive change in our interconnected world.

Globalization is seen by many people as a negative development, as a cause of increasing inequality, affording benefits only to large companies and people who are already wealthy. It is seen as costing jobs in prosperous, developing, and poor countries alike, as a cause of legal and illegal immigration, and as contributing to unemployment and increasing crime rates. The risk is that governments will implement policies that hinder rather than foster globalization.

As I see it, opposition to globalization stems, at least in part, from resistance to the idea of impermanence, of the fact that everything keeps changing at a faster and faster pace. Due to improvements in technology and global communication, changes that used to occur over years or decades now take place in months or days. People are not used to such rapid change. Nevertheless, accepting change as a permanent and inescapable aspect of life is very important.

Dealing constructively with globalization, with all its ups and downs, is one of the most important challenges that companies and governments face. In order to do so, companies and their leaders must learn to embrace the Buddhist principles of impermanence and interdependence and to apply these principles in their decision making.

From Trading Companies to Globally Integrated Organizations

The oldest global companies were, simply put, trading companies: ones that imported and exported goods. At the end of the nineteenth and beginning of the twentieth century, a newer type of global company emerged, as organizations began to build satellite companies in other countries so that they could reduce transportation and import costs and also gain a better understanding of their customers in other parts of the world. Another very important motivation was to avoid being forbidden to export, through pressure by national companies on the government. Although these multinational companies *operated in several countries, the home country was still by far the most important. Today, an increasing number of companies see themselves as globally integrated enterprises, or "citizens of the world." For example, Toyota, though originally a Japanese company, now has plants in twenty-seven countries, including the United States, France, China, and Mexico.*

The Dalai Lama considers the move to globally integrated enterprises a positive one:

The more globally integrated a company, the greater degree of interdependence it can achieve. Consider the three types of companies Laurens mentions above. In trading companies that depend on one another only for import and export, contacts are at arm's length. They involve only buyers and sellers. In multinational companies, the degree of interdependence is greater, as the satellite company is dependent on the parent company in the mother country, and the performance of the parent company is also dependent on the performance of the satellite companies. Communication between the parent company and its satellites is also greater, as they must communicate about production methods, personnel policies, relations with governments, et cetera. The managers and employees from different countries with different cultures have to work effectively together to succeed.

But the globally integrated enterprise is the only type that I would refer to as being based on a "holistic concept." When there is no longer a national parent company with satellites, but a global parent company that claims no home base and rather aims to carry out tasks where they can be executed most efficiently and effectively, regardless of where that might be on the globe, then you have a truly interdependent company. If such a company applies the principles of corporate citizenship or corporate social responsibility discussed in part 2 equally to stakeholders in all countries where it operates, it will have the most impact in correcting the global inequalities that plague today's society.

Of course, as a consequence of interdependence, globally integrated enterprises become both more and less vulnerable at the same time. If one of their factories is destroyed by fire, there is a good chance that another factory can take over the task. That makes the entire company less vulnerable. On the other hand, if there is a fire at a factory in one country, but in order to succeed, a project needs the effective cooperation of factories all over the world, problems arise. In globally integrated companies, all participating units must be able to depend on one another. If one is not performing well, the consequences will be felt by the entire company, increasing vulnerability for all. But this can also be a motivating factor; when people realize that their success depends totally on others, and the other way around, they will feel and act more responsibly. Laurens elaborates:

> *Following Right View means making the decisions that will have the best possible outcome for the company and all its employees and stakeholders. This includes carrying out activities in the locations that lead to the best results for the company as a whole and making decisions from a holistic point of view, considering their impact on employees, shareholders, and other stakeholders in all affected countries. This is a hugely complicated process. Impermanence manifests itself in major changes, like opening and closing factories, setting up additional research facilities in developing countries, and realizing that the best solution next year will not be the same in five years' time. In this context, the principle of looking at decisions from multiple perspectives is very important: from the short, medium, and long term, and in relation to exchanging self for others. For instance, closing a factory may be negative in the short term because it results in the immediate loss of jobs, but may be better for the company*

in the long run. This is unavoidable, a part of impermanence. The task of the leader is to minimize the negative impact of closures. Some irresponsible companies just walk away, whereas responsible organizations make an enormous effort to help people they can no longer employ to find jobs.

For example, a company in Taiwan that had to close a factory but was unable to find work for redundant employees went as far as to start a new activity to provide employment. In Sweden, when a shipyard closed because it could no longer compete with yards in Korea and Japan, the government and the company together developed a program to stimulate entrepreneurship among the employees and to create nonsubsidized, secure employment. This involved training people in how to set up and run a small business. Such actions prevent a negative impact on the image of the company and reduce harm overall.

Strength in Diversity

I see the establishment of harmonious relationships among people of different cultures—races, religious affiliations, tribal identifications, and genders—as one of the most important challenges in the world today. The only way to achieve this, in my view, is to end discrimination and encourage diversity, particularly in the workplace.

Buddha considered respect for all to be very important. Buddhists believe that even if a person acts badly, he or she has the potential to become a good person and deserves respect as a human being. The basis for a harmonious relationship is respect, respect for all people regardless of their cultural background. A Tibetan monk who had been tortured by the Chinese told me, "I could cope with the physical pain. My greatest concern was that I would no longer see the torturer as a fellow human being."

Nelson Mandela expressed the right attitude to cultural diversity in this way:

> On 27 April 1994 the people of South Africa founded a nation on the pledge that we would undo the legacy of our divided past in order to build a better life for all. It was not a pledge that we made lightly. For generations, millions had been deliberately reduced to poverty. . . . For decades we had fought for a non-racial, non-sexist society, and even before we came into power in the historic elections of 1994, our vision of democracy was defined by the principle, among others, that no person or groups of persons shall be subjected to oppression, domination or discrimination by virtue of race, gender, ethnic origin, colour or creed. Once we won power, we chose to regard the diversity of colours and languages that had once been used to divide us as a source of strength.[2]

Cultural diversity is extremely important for globally integrated companies, as they need to be able to communicate and do business with people from a wide range of backgrounds and cultures. This is why having culturally diverse employees is a significant benefit for such companies.

*In 2005, the IBM Corporation, under the leadership of
CEO Samuel Palmisano, was the first company to publicly
announce its application of the "citizen of the world"
concept.[3] It had concluded that innovation was necessary
on a global scale and that the satellite model of a parent
company and dependent subsidiaries was no longer viable.*

*As one example of the way this concept works in
practice, IBM has taken to heart its value statement that
"we are sensitive to the needs of all employees and to the
communities in which we operate." It has developed
detailed responsibility statements throughout its supply
chain, holding its partners to the same high standards set
by its own leaders.*

Palmisano wrote:

> *We know that our company's sizable purchasing
> power is a unique resource that we must manage
> responsibly, and we do. IBM spends nearly $2 bil-
> lion a year with diverse suppliers, for example,
> greater than any other technology company. Yet
> more than managing our spending, we have a re-
> sponsibility to hold ourselves—and our suppliers—
> to high standards of behavior. This means complying
> with all applicable laws and regulations. But it
> goes beyond that. It entails a strong commitment to
> work with suppliers to encourage sound practices
> and develop sound global markets.*

> *We have always maintained an open channel of
> communications with suppliers to set expectations.
> Today, in an increasingly interconnected world*

market, the expectations for all players across the entire supply chain go up. Therefore, we are both reaffirming our existing policies and instituting some new practices, which are spelled out in [our] Supplier Conduct Principles. These principles establish for our suppliers the minimum standards we expect from them as a condition of doing business with IBM. IBM will have the right to take action with suppliers that fail to comply with these principles, including terminating our relationship with them.

Our goal is to work with our suppliers to foster full compliance as they, in turn, apply these to their extended sources of supply engaged in the production of goods and services for IBM. We will consider these principles and adherence to them in our selection process and will seek ongoing compliance by actively monitoring performance.[4]

As the first to embrace the "citizen of the world" concept, IBM has a strong commitment to hiring a diverse workforce. For example, it was the first U.S. company to put European nationals rather than Americans at the head of all its European companies. The rationale for cultural diversity was expressed by Palmisano as follows:

Diversity in IBM is a business imperative. Our customers are diverse; therefore we must understand their diversity by knowing who they are, how they think and what they want. IBM cannot claim that it is dedicated to every client's success unless it

*understands their clients. And those clients cannot
be understood unless IBM has employees from the
same diversity groups.[5]*

*Diversity is also the cornerstone for innovation. According
to IBM studies, 50 percent of GDP growth in the United
States in the second half of the twentieth century was
based on innovation. It used to be that innovation took
place in Western countries and was exported to other parts
of the world. That has changed. Today, innovation has
become global in two ways. First, thanks to the Internet
and to newer and faster systems for distribution, when a
new product comes onto the market it is available globally,
so innovation requires an understanding of the global
marketplace. Second, innovation depends on both insight
and invention, and invention requires as many constructive
innovative inputs as possible. A company with a diverse
workforce can generate far more perspectives and insights
than can a homogeneous group of white men. IBM's
leaders knew that to innovate rapidly, one has to have a
process that is collaborative, multidisciplinary, and global.
They also knew that working effectively across borders
and cultures requires trust between employees and the
people they serve. Such trust can be built only on the
principle of respect for others.*

*Adopting diversity as a goal takes many forms. An
example of IBM's tolerance of different cultural practices
is that as the number of Muslim employees grows, the
company is converting offices in the United States and
Canada into prayer rooms, and restrooms have been*

redesigned to include cleansing stations for Muslim employees' prayer preparation.

GE is another leading global company that sees the world as its home. CEO Jeff Immelt said: "We are committed to performance and to being a good global citizen. . . . Every day we take actions that align our performance ever closer with the standard of what it means to be a good and trusted citizen."[6] GE has come to the same conclusion as IBM, as the following statement shows:

> *GE must become more like their customers. That means more Chinese, more Indians, more Blacks, more women especially in the top ranks.*
>
> *Make no mistake: creating an effective and harmonious workforce populated by people from different backgrounds is a huge challenge. But it is a necessary one for companies that wish to compete in today's globalized world.*

We have to face the reality that discrimination exists. For centuries, people have been subjugated or treated unfairly simply because of their race, gender, background, or ethnic group. It takes time to eradicate those prejudices. But I believe that not only can it be done, it must be done—and that it is up to today's business leaders to take the first steps.

Competition Is a Means to an End

Another positive result of globalization is increasing competition. Competition generates a very powerful force to produce what people want at reasonable prices. But it is a means; it is not an end. The end is to generate benefits for all. So why is it so difficult to arrive at fair competition and an equitable distribution of those benefits?

Competition generates wealth. But if leaders of businesses are interested only in enriching themselves as fast as possible, with little or no regard for any harmful consequences to others, then competition is being used in the wrong way.

> *If we disregard such obviously bad actions as selling dangerous products or making dishonest claims about a product, some of the most harmful competitive practices are establishing a monopoly position and price fixing. These practices are illegal in most countries but are still widespread.*
>
> *Governments themselves are also involved in distorting competition, especially at the global level, by subsidizing their national companies and establishing trade barriers to protect these companies from competition. Most subsidies in prosperous countries are now applied in the agricultural sector, but governments face the problem that if they radically reduce these protections in a short span of time, this can lead to a high level of unemployment.*
>
> *Another activity that leads to unfair competition is lobbying of government officials by business. Businesses have a right and a duty to inform government about the effect a policy the government wishes to implement will have on their businesses. But often, businesses consider the impact of a policy for the public at large only from their*

own point of view. This is clearly an example of adopting
a self-centered perspective, of wrong view.

One more point on competition: many people see only
competition and do not realize that competition and
cooperation can coexist. The ability of a company to
compete depends on effective cooperation among all its
employees, and with its partners and suppliers. In
addition, even many competitors cooperate in areas such
as setting safety and performance standards. Unfair and
dishonest competition does take place, but it is possible to
compete while respecting ethical standards.

When we face reality, it is obvious that we cannot imagine a modern society without competition as a fact of life. I do not claim that in this book we outline all the answers to making competition work effectively for everyone. I do believe, however, that following many of the suggestions we have already made about Right View and Right Conduct can help today's leaders create a more positive form of competition. Along those lines, I believe that the teachings of Buddhism and the principles of Right View and Right Conduct can also be applied to solving the world's environmental problems.

Meeting the Environmental Challenge

The challenge for global companies is to help make the world a better place. This is increasingly difficult, as the combination of rapid growth in population and increases in the standard of

living is threatening the viability of our planet. Global companies, particularly globally integrated enterprises, are in an ideal
position to meet these challenges. Global companies not only
have the most resources to solve environmental problems, but
it is also in their best interests to use them. Here are some examples:

Wind Turbines in India[7]

> Tulsi Tanti, an Indian engineer, managed and owned a
> small textile company. When he saw his profits being
> reduced by regular failures in the electricity supply, he
> bought two wind turbines to generate power and solve the
> problem. Then, in 2000, he read about global warming. As
> he said: "I suddenly had a very clear vision. If Indians
> start consuming power like Americans the world will run
> out of resources. Either you stop India developing, or you
> find some alternate solution." That is an example of Right
> View; he saw the impact of his decisions and actions not
> only on his own well-being but on the well-being of others.
>   So, in an example of Right Conduct, Tanti sold his
> textile company and entered the wind turbine business. By
> 2007 he had become the fourth-largest wind turbine maker
> in the world, with revenues of $850 million. He
> commented: "Yes, green business is good business. But it's
> not just about making a profit. It's about being
> responsible." He started by selling wind turbines but soon
> realized that the buyers were not really interested in wind
> turbines: he knew that businesses would buy them anyway
> because they wanted a reliable energy supply. He changed

his business model to sell energy instead and organized financing, installation, and maintenance himself. Without this innovation, he would never have succeeded as he did.

Tanti pulled off an incredible feat by buying a German wind turbine producer, RE Power, for $1.7 billion. The French company AREVA—one of the most powerful power companies in the world, controlled by the French government, managed by one of the best managers in France, and with revenues of $13.7 billion—already owned 30 percent of REpower. Tanti said: "I can take a company with a 4 percent profit margin and turn it into a company with a 20 percent margin. AREVA can't. So I knew from the beginning: whatever they offered, I could pay more."[8] That illustrates a saying of Buddha: "The greatest treasure man can have is self-confidence."

Now Tanti runs a truly global company: the power stations are designed in the Netherlands, the turbines are manufactured in Germany, and the heavy steelwork and installation are handled in India. The well-being of all those involved has improved. The reason Tanti is exceptionally successful in India is the poor functioning of the country's electricity supply. Getting a reliable energy supply justifies paying a higher price than would be the case if India had a reliable power delivery system.

Carbon Credits in an Outcast Community[9]

Another example from India shows how globalization can reduce global warming, while at the same time helping to move subsistence farmers from abject poverty to a decent standard of living. The organizations involved are the World Bank, a paper mill, a small Indian NGO, and an innovative leader with the right thinking and the right motivation.

In one of the poorest areas in India, where half the people belong to the lowest caste, the "untouchables" or outcasts, and the illiteracy rate is 90 percent, people live in chronic poverty and are barely able to feed themselves enough to survive. Yet until now, 60 percent of their land, the most valuable resource they have, was uncultivated because they lacked the knowledge and capital needed to farm on it. That gave Masabathula Satyanarayana, a leader with a forestry background, an idea. Under his scheme, the farmers would plant trees on the uncultivated land, selling the trees to the paper mill to finance the buying of the plants (the farmers would plant new trees to replace those they cut down). Then, in a long and difficult process, Satyanarayana convinced the World Bank (over objections that the management of the project was too weak) to pay the farmers carbon credits for the carbon the trees produced. The scheme, which took four years to get off the ground, will eventually increase forest coverage on 3,500 hectares (around 8,500 acres) and provide an escape from abject poverty for three thousand subsistence farmers.

The plan never would have succeeded without the leadership of Masabathula Satyanarayana. The project leader said:

These farmers have always been poor, so were their ancestors. If you experiment and it goes wrong

there's no cushion, it's a disaster. We have to spend
a long time building their confidence, demonstrat-
ing how it will work.

Finally, to make the project really attractive the
World Bank had to be convinced to award carbon
credits that could be sold. That was also a long and
difficult process and came close to failure because
the World Bank feared that the management capa-
bilities in the project were too weak. Perseverance,
vigor, humility, generosity, and self-confidence — all
qualities of a mindful leader — saved the project.[10]

Examples such as these are encouraging, but much more still
has to be done to avoid environmental catastrophe. We are all responsible for what happens and will happen in the world. Leaders of global companies who accept this universal responsibility
can make a contribution far greater than the products they sell
and the direct benefits they deliver to their employees, clients,
shareholders, and other stakeholders. Organizations and governments together can play an important role in helping to solve
environmental problems and in improving the well-being of
others, not only in their own countries but throughout the
world.

8

Entrepreneurship and Poverty

Poverty is a huge problem all over the world. But I believe that poverty is, at least in part, a problem of the mind. If all people, organizations, and governments applied the principles of Right View and Right Conduct, much of the world's poverty could be eliminated.

Four conditions are necessary to make such rapid progress. First, the government of a country must be motivated to improve the well-being of all citizens and not only of an economic elite or of the members of government. Second, the economic system has to be developed along the principles of a responsible free-market economy (described in chapter 9). Third, regulations must stimulate entrepreneurship. Finally, voluntary family planning has to be introduced more successfully to reduce the rate of population growth.

As a consequence, the population will shift from agriculture to manufacturing and service, the cities will grow, and the number of people living in rural areas and working in agriculture will decline. In many countries, extreme poverty is concentrated in rural areas. It is impossible to solve the poverty problem without people moving from the countryside to cities. This can, however, be achieved only if people can find decent jobs in the cities. This transition requires the acceptance of impermanence by all citizens. If people are not willing to move and change jobs, it is impossible to solve the poverty problem. The same applies to family size, which I will discuss later in this chapter.

Making economic progress depends on "adding value," which is the primary goal of an entrepreneur. As we saw in the example about reforestation in the previous chapter, when subsistence farmers produced trees in addition to food, their prosperity increased. If poor farmers continue to work as they do now, they will remain poor forever. Ingenuity can add value, but in most cases the budding entrepreneur also needs capital. If in the reforestation case the farmer had not been able to borrow money based on the contract with the paper mill, the project would have failed.

Entrepreneurship can also add value by creating jobs. For example, a woman who stitches dresses by hand in a poor country will be very poor. But if she buys a sewing machine, she can produce more and will earn more. And if she earns more, she can hire people to work for her, who can in turn sew more dresses, increasing her profit further. It is a very simple process. The more jobs are created, the more value is added — and vice versa.

Buddha recognized entrepreneurship as a valuable activity. He encouraged entrepreneurs to be successful by being reliable and having an eye for what would sell. He also suggested they save money for a rainy day and share some of the results with their employees. Remember, according to Buddhism, our first responsibility is to take care of ourselves; only then can we begin to care for others. Entrepreneurship is an excellent way to be able to take care of oneself and others by enhancing our standard of living. Entrepreneurship is by far the most effective method to enable people to earn more, and in turn they will consume more and become participating members of the economy. This improves the standard of living for everyone, which is why it is in the best interests of companies and organizations to stimulate and encourage entrepreneurship whenever possible. This is the Right View.

No matter what part of the world we come from, we are all human beings. We all want happiness and try to avoid suffering. We have the same basic human needs and concerns. All human beings want freedom and the right to determine their destiny as individuals and as peoples, and in order to do so, we need the opportunity to rise above abject poverty. It is human nature to want such things, and it is within our power to provide them.

Shifting Perspective

After becoming independent in 1947, India pursued a policy of self-sufficiency and import substitution, meaning that instead of importing products it developed its own industries to build the domestic economy. This policy was very heavily regulated; the government determined which products would be produced and where they would be manufactured within the country. Very little business activity could take place without the initiative or approval of a government department in Delhi, otherwise known as the "license raj" system. This restrictive policy (and some other factors) led to a financial crisis in 1991, at which time the government asked Manmohan Singh, a Sikh with a PhD in economics from Oxford, to become minister of finance. Dr. Singh accepted and very quickly diagnosed the problem: the system was stifling entrepreneurship. He told the prime minister:

> *We are on the verge of an economic collapse. It is possible that we will collapse, but there is a chance that if we take bold measures we may turn around, and turn it into an opportunity. We must convert this crisis into an opportunity to build a new India.[1]*

Dr. Singh then told the parliament:

> *Victor Hugo said, "No power on earth can stop an idea whose time has come." We can follow the traditional way, tighten our belts, tighten and tighten, but if we do that it will lead to more misery and more unemployment. There is an alternative path. The idea whose time has come is that India should emerge as a major global and economic power. This alternative path is economic stabilization and a "credible structural adjustment program."*

What was this "credible structural adjustment program"? The program consisted of abandoning the policy of import substitution and opening India to imports, encouraging entrepreneurship along the way. In Dr. Singh's words:

> *We got the government off the backs of the people of India, particularly off the backs of India's*

entrepreneurs. We introduced competition, both internal competition and external competition. We made risk-taking much more attractive and much more profitable. So we tried to create an environment conducive to the growth of business. We removed a large number of controls and regulations, which in the past had stifled the spirit of innovation and the spirit of entrepreneurship, and restructured the scope of competition, both internal and external. As the result, in the '90s productivity increase in the Indian industry has been much faster than ever before.

Although the details at the time were slim, Dr. Singh said afterward in an interview:

My dream was that as we were in a crisis, that we should undertake basic structural changes. Out of that would emerge a new India, an India where there will be no poverty, the freedom from poverty, ignorance, and disease. You get that with India becoming a major global player in the world economy. That was the vision that inspired our economic reforms.

Dr. Singh had presented a vital policy change: relying on entrepreneurs and not on government departments to create jobs, and recognizing that in order to achieve that, entrepreneurs need freedom. He also identified the critical elements without which none of this would succeed:

provisions for making it easy to start a business in a legal way, securing property rights, and ensuring judicial independence and impartial courts. We will return to these points later in this chapter.

The economic reforms that Dr. Singh referred to were heavily influenced by what he had observed happening in South Korea. South Korea had started from a similar position to India's in 1950. Along with some other East Asian countries, it had succeeded in one generation in transforming the character of its economy, eradicating chronic poverty in the process. South Korea put more emphasis on basic education and health care, priorities that have not taken hold in India's transformation.

In his exile in India, the Dalai Lama witnessed the country's development firsthand.

Dr. Singh changed the economic policies that had been established by Nehru, the first prime minister after India became free. I met Nehru several times and was always impressed by his kindness, in word and action, for us Tibetans, as exiles in his country. He also gave me the impression of being a highly intelligent person with the interest of all Indians at heart, and so I interpret his role in the economic crisis as one with good motivation.

Dr. Singh provides an excellent example of what we could call "the ability to shift perspective," or to view a problem from different angles, a true sign of a mindful leader. Dr. Singh saw reality as it was and recognized the impermanence of India's economic situation—what had worked when India first became a free nation was no longer working. As a result, he was able to change a negative situation into a positive opportunity. Because he was not acting out of self-centeredness, but out of concern for the good of the entire Indian society, he was able to look at a situation from different points of view: the personal level, the community level, the national level; the personal perspective, the economic perspective, the government perspective, the business perspective; and a short- and long-term vantage point.

Of course, when you have a crisis that is global in nature, such as environmental degradation or problems in the economic structure, a coordinated and concerted effort among many people is an absolute necessity. But change must start from within the individual. For individual leaders, finding solutions requires a flexible and supple mind. When facing a problem like Dr. Singh's, the leader needs not only a very high level of knowledge and competence, but also the ability to identify the Right View—and then to act on it.

Helping Entrepreneurship to Flourish

Two of the necessary conditions for stimulating entrepreneurship are that governments have the right motivation and that they establish and implement the right regulations. These two aspects are linked. For example, a government with the wrong motivation will not establish the right regulations; and indeed, in such countries you may find government officials living in luxury in the midst of widespread poverty. The right motivation means that the government sees its role as looking after the well-being of all the citizens of the country, especially the poor.

Facilitating Business Start-ups

It sounds strange, but the fact is that it is much more difficult for an entrepreneur to start a business in a poor country than in a prosperous one. In many poor countries it is almost impossible for an entrepreneur to set up a business in a legal way: it takes too long, is too complicated, and costs far more than they can afford. The only way is to operate in the black market, and indeed, in many poor countries the black market is greater in size than the official market. The facts are well known, but governments in poor countries have great difficulty changing the law, often because of the self-interest and at times corruption of economic and professional elites who make their money from giving approvals for business start-ups—lawyers, professional institutions, and a large number of government departments that all want to be paid, officially and often unofficially.

A government must have the courage, self-confidence, and lack of fear to face down vested interest groups like an economic elite and to act in the interests of society at large. The preoccupation of professionals and government employees with the resulting loss of income can be understood, but their situation will be much better once the economy starts to flourish through successful entrepreneurship. Lawyers and accountants are well paid in prosperous countries, after all.

Securing Property Rights

Secure property rights are very important for stimulating investment and facilitating entrepreneurship. Secure property rights—that an owned property cannot be arbitrarily taken away—may seem like a given for those in most Western nations, but this isn't the case in many parts of the world. In China, for example, it used to be that all land and production belonged to the state, and the state could repossess homes and households at its whim. But, once it moved to a system where farmers could obtain a thirty-year lease and sell a portion of their product in the "free" market, there has been a significant increase in output, about half of which is ascribed to the changes in land rights.

Anybody visiting a large city in a poor country will notice the slums on its outskirts. The people living there are very poor and are likely to have moved from rural areas to the city to find work. They start living in the most primitive conditions on open land, where it is not clear if anybody has property rights or not.

Electricity and water companies are often not willing to provide these basic services to those without property rights. In addition, such people are at the mercy of low-level community employees who demand bribes to allow the poor to stay where they are. If the government or community decides to give rights to the minuscule plot to the family living there, the status of those people changes dramatically for the better. And when they are owners, it is beneficial for them to improve their very rudimentary dwellings.

This change can be more powerful than providing microcredit (on which there is more to follow)—the value of these small plots is far in excess of the size of a microcredit loan and offers many other benefits.[2] But implementing such a change demands courage from the government, since many people both inside and outside government profit from these poor people's lack of basic security.

The problem of property rights is not limited to private entitlements but also extends to the property rights of business, or intellectual property. Many companies do not believe that the courts will uphold their property rights; in fact, a 2005 study by the World Bank concluded that businesspeople in Indonesia, Tanzania, India, Pakistan, Brazil, Poland, Russia, and Peru had very low confidence in obtaining a fair interpretation of the law, in most cases lower than 50 percent.[3] The World Bank found this lack of confidence to be related to the time required to enforce a contract. In Pakistan and Brazil the process of enforcing property rights could take years and considerable financial resources.[4]

I visited a government office dealing with property rights in Jaipur in India. The files were stacked three meters high and three meters deep without any space between the stacks. With such a system it is impossible to find out what the rights for a particular property are. The only people who can find out are those who can pay for an

official to start digging. Fortunately, the Indian
government has solved this problem. These deeds are being
computerized, and anyone can ask to see them for a very
low standard fee.

Giving title to land, houses, and ideas has a very positive impact
on reducing poverty, increasing investment, and creating jobs—
and yet progress is slow. Governments must be very determined
to carry out such entitlement programs and to oversee judicial
systems to uphold them.

Having a Fair, Functioning Banking System

In 1991, when I first visited Dharamsala, India, where the
Dalai Lama has his residence, the state bank of India had
only one branch. It was open for four hours a day, five
days a week, and every day at 4:00 p.m. there was still a
line outside waiting to be served. As you can imagine, such
a poorly functioning banking system was a huge obstacle
for entrepreneurs wanting to do business. Today, the
system has changed completely. There are now several
private banks, and you can change currency eighteen
hours a day, seven days a week—and many small
businesses flourish.

A banking system that includes microlending or
microcredit has proven extremely effective in helping small
businesses, because it allows for the extension of small
loans to entrepreneurs too poor to qualify for traditional
bank loans.[5]

Microcredit is an ethical business practice. Unlike

typical lending practices, which promote the self-interest
of the lender, microlending serves the best interest of
society at large. Therefore, it is consistent with Right
Conduct. For example:

- *It recognizes and promotes credit as a human right.*
- *It is not based on any collateral or contracts, but rather on*
  trust between the parties involved.
- *Its goal is to keep interest rates at low levels, rather than*
  to achieve high returns for lenders and investors.[6]

In short, microcredit is based on the idea that the poor
have skills that are underused, and that it is not for lack of
skills that people end up poor; it is for lack of opportunity.
Microcredit is also based on the premise that poor people
are trustworthy and diligent about paying back their
loans. Breaking down the stereotype that the poor are
unskilled and unreliable is one of the most critical steps in
the fight against poverty.

Over the past three decades, Muhammad Yunus and the
Grameen Bank of Bangladesh have used microcredit to
ameliorate the plight of the poor worldwide. The concept
has been so successful that Professor Yunus and the bank
were jointly awarded the Nobel Peace Prize in 2006, with
the recognition that "lasting peace cannot be achieved
unless large population groups find ways in which to
break out of poverty. Micro-credit is one such means."

Some people make the mistake of thinking that
microcredit alone can solve the problem of poverty;
however, microcredit is only one component. For

*entrepreneurship to flourish, the entire banking system
must be fair, efficient, and open to all.*

*Another organization that takes the concept of
microcredit but expands on it is BRAC, established by
Fazle Hasan Abed in 1972 to help Bangladesh overcome
the devastation caused by the war with West Pakistan.
BRAC's objectives are "poverty alleviation and
empowerment of the poor." While the organization believes
that microcredit is an important tool for breaking the
poverty cycle, it also trains its members in income
generation and helps them link to markets for their goods.
Its holistic approach begins with women as the primary
caregivers and combines microcredit with health,
education, and other social development programs.*

*BRAC's Economic Development program organizes
almost five million poor people, mostly women, and has
operations in around a dozen countries, including
countries in Africa and the Middle East, as well as
Afghanistan and Sri Lanka. In addition to the provision
of credit and savings accounts, there are human rights and
legal education courses, legal aid clinics, and household
visits by volunteer health workers. The Health, Nutrition,
and Population program provides more than ninety-seven
million people with basic health services, including control
of infectious diseases such as tuberculosis, acute
respiratory infections, and diarrhea, and advice on
preventive health measures. The aim of poverty reduction
through education is addressed by the Non Formal
Primary Education program, which has almost fifty
thousand schools containing a high proportion of those*

traditionally excluded from formal schooling, particularly
girls. The Adolescent Development program gives training
in vocational skills, health awareness, including
reproductive health, and leadership.[7]

Reducing the Rate of Population Growth

In 2002, I joined 136 other spiritual leaders from thirty-one
countries—Roman Catholic, Protestant, Muslim, and Hindu—in
sending a letter to President Bush to encourage him to continue
to provide funding for the voluntary family planning provided
by the United Nations Population Fund (UNFPA). I wrote in that
letter, "Family planning is crucial, especially in the developing
world." Another Nobel Peace Prize winner, South African Arch-
bishop Desmond Tutu, wrote, "Planned parenthood is an obligation of those who are Christians. Our church thinks we should
use scientific methods that assist in planning families."[8]

This is not only an economic issue. It is a question of freedom
and the right of women to be able to decide how many children
they wish to have and when. No man has a right to force a
woman to have a child that is not welcome.

In Buddhism we consider every life to be precious. However, the population explosion is ultimately a very serious matter. So family planning is crucial, especially in the developing
world.[9]

When you read in the newspapers about the ravages of
illness, natural disasters, internal wars, HIV/AIDS, and
lack of food in poor countries, you might expect that the
population there is stagnating or even declining. The

opposite is in fact the case: the poorer the country, the faster the population growth.

I will try to illustrate this with a few examples. The United States has the highest rate of population growth among prosperous countries. In 2006 it had a population of 300 million. That is the same as Pakistan, the Congo, and Ethiopia added together. Assuming that the birthrate (the average number of children per woman) remains the same in each country, by 2050 the U.S. population will have grown to 420 million. The other three countries together will have increased to 690 million, that is, 270 million more than the United States.

What about other statistics relating to the same three developing countries? Infant mortality — that is, the number of children who die under the age of one per one thousand live births — is eighty, so eight out of every one hundred children die within their first year. Life expectancy is forty-six years. And 80 percent of the population in these countries lives on less than $2 per day. [10]

All these countries have inadequate infrastructures — poor roads, power that is available only intermittently, lack of safe drinking water and no sewage system, insufficient schools, hospitals, and medical doctors. They all need to make huge investments in these areas, as well as in training and paying for qualified teachers and doctors to provide their people with a decent standard of living and to bring down infant mortality rates and increase life expectancy substantially. As the population grows, so does the size of the investment needed. Even

wealthy countries with low rates of population growth
have difficulty financing their infrastructure and health-
care requirements.

Let us look at another example. In 2006 there were 60
million people in the UK and 75 million in Ethiopia. In
2050 the UK will have 70 million inhabitants and Ethiopia
145 million, that is, more than England and France
combined. Think what would happen if the population of
the UK doubled by 2050.

China has been very successful in reducing its birthrate
per woman, which was down to 1.6 in 2006. However, to
do this it employed what some regard as extreme
measures, limiting couples to one child. A second
pregnancy may result in a fine, "encouragement" to have
an abortion, or even forced sterilization. In contrast, a
very poor state in India reduced its birthrate as fast as
China did by using education rather than coercion. Kerala
is a large district with approximately 35 million
inhabitants. The birthrate was reduced from 4.4 in the
1950s to 1.8 in 1991. How did Kerala achieve this? Four
actions were taken: encouraging good basic health care,
allowing many women to work, encouraging men to
respect women, and promoting open and informed public
discussion. The important variables are education, job
opportunity, and nondiscrimination against women. The
conclusion is that birthrates can be reduced without
coercion, but doing so requires major changes in attitudes
and values. The Right View is that each couple should aim
to have no more than two children for the world
population to be at a sustainable level.

The Dalai Lama is very concerned about poverty and about the risk that the world might run out of natural resources. He considers life to be holy but is convinced that in the situation the world, and poor countries in particular, face today, it is absolutely necessary to reduce the birthrate.

Fortunately, governments in practically all very poor countries consider their birthrates too high. However, they have difficulty doing anything about it. The Dalai Lama considers it very important that a reduction be achieved only by using peaceful means, that is, by convincing men and women to reduce family size voluntarily. Kerala's example is one that many countries may find beneficial to follow. Reducing the birthrate does not require a large investment—it is a question of education and a change in attitude.

Collaboration between Business and Government

Solving the problems of poverty requires a combination of action by central and local government, contributions from prosperous countries, and help from responsible global companies. South Korea has demonstrated that a country can be successful in eliminating poverty in one generation if the government is competent and in charge of the transformation process. Only a national government can establish an environment in which entrepreneurship will flourish, raising the impoverished out of unacceptable conditions.

Global companies with the right motivation can find ways to act that are simultaneously beneficial for their companies, the countries in which they operate, and also the poor. I am in favor of wealthy people and companies contributing to charities. But it is clear to me that much faster change can be achieved when a company finds ways to create employment and stimulate entrepreneurship among the poor. While a charitable donation can sometimes go some way, it is finite. But helping people to expand their own businesses will allow them to increase their profit and grow indefinitely. And when this occurs, the company too will profit from the additional value it has helped create within that society. Here are some examples of how businesses can help the poor to earn a decent living and add value to the economy at the same time.

Shakti in India

Unilever, a global supplier of nutritional and personal care products, reaches customers around the globe every day. Beyond this basic business objective, the company views two other goals as important: creating wealth for the company and for society and minimizing the negative environmental impact of its operations.[11] Unilever has recognized that stimulating entrepreneurship among the poor is essential to creating wealth and reducing poverty. In particular, the company has recognized that creating entrepreneurs and jobs in India, Indonesia, and other developing countries is beneficial to the company as well as to society: reduced poverty in those countries means more people can afford to buy Unilever's products.

The challenge for Unilever in expanding its market in India was figuring out how to reach millions of potential consumers in small, remote villages where there is no retail distribution network, no advertising coverage, and poor roads and transport. The solution was Project Shakti ("shakti" means "strength" in Hindi), launched in 2000 in conjunction with nongovernmental organizations, micro-lending banks, and local governments. In many of the villages, women have formed self-help groups. Unilever made a presentation of its Shakti scheme to these self-help groups to find women who wanted to become entrepreneurs.

The easiest way to understand how Shakti works is by looking at an example. Rojamma, from a very poor family, was married at seventeen to a man with whom she had two daughters but who then left her to fend for herself. She earned a few rupees working in her mother's field but found it almost impossible to survive. Unilever made a presentation to her self-help group offering members the opportunity to sell and deliver the company's products in her village. Rojamma accepted the job.

Under Project Shakti, Unilever provides training in sales and bookkeeping to help women like Rojamma become full-fledged microentrepreneurs. The company then helped her borrow ten thousand rupees (two hundred U.S. dollars) at favorable conditions to invest in a stock of goods to start up her business. Rojamma visits her clients carrying products to sell. The target is to have about five hundred customers. She sells about ten thousand rupees' worth of Unilever's goods per month and makes a profit of about eight hundred rupees per month (sixteen U.S.

dollars; average agricultural wage rates for women in India are 30–40 rupees a day). But this job has given her more than just the means to support herself and her family; it has also helped her achieve a greater sense of self-respect. Rojamma said, "When my husband left me I had nothing except my daughters. Today everyone knows me. I am someone. It also has enabled me to send my daughters to school, a chance I did not have."

In 2006, the system was operating effectively in fifty thousand villages and involved over thirty thousand women. Unilever's goal is to establish one hundred thousand Shakti entrepreneurs by 2010, reaching six hundred million people in five hundred thousand villages.[12]

Innovating for the Common Good

Clearly, global companies can be quite successful in reducing poverty and stimulating entrepreneurship in developing countries. But in many cases, this cannot happen without the cooperation of central and local governments.

Indonesia is very populous, with a population of 225 million that will rise to 285 million in 2050 and a birthrate of 2.4. Around 50 percent of the population lives on less than US$2 per day.

Oxfam, a prominent NGO, and Unilever decided to carry out a joint project to evaluate the impact of Unilever's activities on reducing poverty.[13] *Oxfam approached this with a positive but skeptical attitude about how effective the activities of global companies* could be. Yet each recognized the other as a serious organization, and there was mutual respect.

The study took more than a year and examined the impact of everything from Unilever's relationships with small-scale producers to its interactions with low-income consumers to its employment policies and practices, as well as the wider impact on the community.[14] Once the study was concluded, both organizations had a much better understanding of the limitations and opportunities that determine what companies can and cannot be expected to do to reduce poverty in developing countries.

The study found that "of the total value created, around two-thirds is distributed to participants other than Unilever Indonesia, such as producers, suppliers, distributors, retailers and the Indonesian government." However, it concluded:

> Participation in value chains such as Unilever Indonesia's does not automatically guarantee improvements in the lives of people living in poverty. For supply and distribution chains to benefit poor people even more, there need to be other social institutions and resources in place such as credit and saving schemes, marketing associations, and insurance schemes.

Oxfam stated:

> Many companies still see their purpose as profit maximisation, but we have learned from Unilever that in many cases business decisions rarely amount

to a strictly profit-based calculation. The notion
that the business of business is business is outdated.
There are huge opportunities to innovate for the
common good.

This is an example of both Oxfam and Unilever, which
began from different perspectives, facing reality. They
wanted to find out the truth, and they both overcame their
fear that it would have a negative effect on their
reputations.

When thinking about Unilever's relationships in India and Indonesia in terms of the Right View and the concept of interdependence, these findings become quite obvious. There are many interdependent pieces of society—governments, banks, global companies, and individual entrepreneurs—that must all work together to achieve the goal of reducing poverty. It is one-sided to look only at the profit Unilever is making; the other participants also play an interdependent and equally important role. This is why it is instructive to look at what governments can do to help stimulate entrepreneurship and help lift people out of poverty.

Regulation and Freedom

On the surface, freedom and regulation may seem to be opposing concepts. But what might be a limitation for some is actually a freedom for others. For example, the very strict regulations that a pharmaceutical company must follow before it is allowed to

sell a new drug impose many limitations on a business. Pharmaceutical companies are required by law to wait five to ten years
after discovering a new drug before selling the product to the
public. During these five to ten years, the drug must be tested on
a large number of people. From the company's point of view this
is a limitation, but from the consumer's point of view this is very
good, because it allows him or her to be free from worry that the
drug might be dangerous. The fact that regulations always impose limitations on some while granting freedom to others is
probably why it is so difficult to develop regulations that please
everybody. But I firmly believe that companies and governments
must put the good of the general public first when enacting
regulations—even if it means imposing limitations on certain
individuals or groups. Remember, the Right View looks at the
consequences of one's actions and decisions from many perspectives and chooses the action that will benefit the most and
harm the fewest.

As Buddhists, we rarely consider limits to freedom. We believe
that when people have the right motivation, they will not abuse
their freedom. When we speak about freedom, we are thinking
primarily of freeing ourselves from bad habits, negative thoughts,
and bad motivations. Yet not everyone thinks about freedom in
this way. I recognize that countries need laws to set limits to freedom, or chaos will ensue. I think, however, that it should not be
forgotten that many of these laws set limits that would not be
crossed by people acting responsibly. Acting responsibly requires more than not breaking the law. I have been pleased to
note that several companies in their business principles state that
they will respect not only the letter but also the spirit of the law.

Most people want maximum freedom. But unlimited freedom

is not only impossible; it is dangerous. Total freedom would mean that whoever is the strongest decides, whether their view is right or wrong. And when the strong can exert their will upon the weak, the end result is less freedom for all.

The Buddhist view is that all people should have the same rights to justice and a decent standard of living regardless of their place in society. This would be true in a perfect world, if everyone acted according to Right View and Right Conduct. But Buddhists accept that in reality there are a large number of people who will not act according to Right View and Right Conduct. That is why it is necessary to have regulations to protect the freedoms of those with less influence or power.

But as hard as we may try to reduce the inequality and injustice in the world—be it economic, political, or social—injustices still exist. And these are the cause of most of the world's problems. Whether it is suffering due to poverty in one part of the world or the denial of freedom and basic human rights in another part, we should never perceive these events in total isolation. Eventually, their repercussions will be felt everywhere.

The world is getting smaller, and everything depends on everything else. Others' interests are actually our own interests as well. If others are happy, we will be happy. If others suffer, we ultimately will suffer.[15]

This is why it is important for organizations—whether they be corporate, nonprofit, or even governmental—to take a leadership role in addressing the huge economic imbalances. I believe the time has now come to address all these global issues from the perspective of the oneness of humanity, and from a profound understanding of the deeply interconnected nature of today's world.[16]

9

The Responsible Free-Market Economy

The basic human desire for freedom and happiness cannot be subdued. The thousands of people who marched in the cities of Eastern Europe a few decades ago, the unwavering determination of the people in my homeland of Tibet, and the recent demonstrations in Burma are all powerful reminders of this truth. As discussed in chapter 8, freedom is a necessary precondition for creativity and human development. It is not enough, as communist systems once assumed, to provide people with food, shelter, and clothing. If we have these things but lack the liberty to sustain our deeper nature and realize our full potential, we remain only half human.[1]

A democratic system based on freedom is, in my view, the only system that can bring us our collective happiness without risking a serious abuse of power. Here I am talking about functioning democracies, not one-party democracies or one-leader-forever democracies or democracies where the country is in a state of chaos. A real democracy creates checks and balances within the government, so that if a leader is found to have bad motivation or be incompetent, the system can counter the problem. It makes the government aware that its task is to serve the people, not the other way around, and to act responsibly in the process.

A democracy has the added advantage of being able to hold public debates in which everyone is free to express his or her opinion. As a result, people are better informed and are free from manipulation or coercion by the government. Buddha attached great significance to freedom and emphasized the importance of free choice and responsibility. Buddha also repeatedly stressed the importance of discipline; he believed that only through discipline can we free ourselves from negative thoughts and emotions. In other words, discipline is the key to making the right decisions.

In The Leader's Way, *we have been talking about how individual leaders can develop new skills and train their minds for more disciplined decision making. We have considered the role of such a mindful leader, how he or she can shape the values and the agenda of an organization. We have also seen how leading companies are making strides in the areas of corporate responsibility, environmental sustainability, and the fight against poverty. All this exists under the scope of varying economic and political systems.*

In the many discussions I have had with the Dalai Lama about the economic and political systems in which visionary leaders and organizations could best thrive, he emphasized that the most successful system should be a democratic system based on freedom, but also on compassion and concern for the well-being of all those within its scope. Such a system, as the Dalai Lama came to realize, has the most potential to exist under the umbrella of the free market.

Socialism and the Free Market

For much of my life, I was attracted to the socialist or communist system because I understood its objective as to provide a decent standard of living and justice for all. I was drawn to it for its equality; in such a system, extreme differences in standards of living between people are not to be tolerated. The stated objectives of socialist systems include abolishing poverty and furthering the brotherhood among people and among countries, which I, of course, found very appealing. But over time, I found out that the countries that practiced the communist system did not reach this objective; they did not even try to. On the contrary, I found that by suppressing free markets and individual freedoms like freedom of speech and freedom to own property, these systems were actually stagnating development and furthering poverty and hardship. Although I still believe that the initial objective was right, I have come to see the flaws in such a system.

My understanding of the communist system was deepened through the meetings I had with China's communist chairman, Mao Tse-tung. In person, Mao impressed me in many ways. When he first explained the communist system to me, I did not realize that it was a command-and-control system based on central planning of economic activity. He explained it as a system where the capitalists would no longer exploit the workers, which I fully supported. It was not initially obvious to me that the abolition of private ownership would lead to ownership by the state, with a party elite in charge who would then institute their own restrictive command-and-control system and rule as an elite, like the aristocracies in the past. Of course, we now know this led to many human rights abuses.

Once, Mao invited me to attend a meeting with his cabinet. What I especially remember was that when he asked the cabinet members for suggestions on how they could improve the performance of the government, the room went silent. Nobody said a word. Mao then pulled out a letter he had received that described many serious problems the people were facing, leaving me with the impression that he had a sincere interest in the well-being of the Chinese people. He came across as a great leader and, for some time, I admired him. What finally changed my mind was that he told me that religion is like poison. He knew that I was a Buddhist, so his comments made clear to me that the friendship he had shown was not genuine.

It is through this process of listening and observing that I have come to put my faith in the free-market system. Although it has great potential for abuses as well, the fact that it allows for freedom and diversity of thought and religion has convinced me that it is the one we should be working from. Of course, I still believe we should strive for an adequate standard of living for all rather than the "survival of the fittest" position that the free market often follows. The recent developments in China demonstrate how even small movements toward a free-market system can boost economic development and help lift people out of poverty. But of course, in the case of China there is still much work to be done. Laurens explains:

> *Almost all modern governments have chosen variants of the free-market system; the pure command-and-control economies have all but gone by the wayside. Nevertheless, the issue is not as straightforward as merely choosing a system, as in the case of China.*
>
> *In the past few decades, China has put its economic goals above its political ones. Its leaders abandoned the communist policies of central planning and control, and reduced state ownership of the means of production. The country identified four areas for modernization: agriculture, industry, the military, and science and technology.[2] In agriculture, rural communities were discontinued and peasants were allowed to lease land and sell their harvest in markets. Special economic zones, such as Shenzhen and Xiamen, were created, where foreign investment was encouraged and new factories were established. The military was modernized by reducing the number of soldiers and improving military technology with advanced weapons systems. To boost science and technology, thousands of students were sent abroad, particularly to the United States, to study science and engineering.*
>
> *Although China has continued to implement free-market policies with great economic success, it has come under increased scrutiny in recent years for human rights issues. Despite these steps in the right direction, the country's regulatory and monetary policies are not yet at*

the same level as other free-market economies. In other words, China demonstrates a marriage of a Communist Party–based government with a free-market economy. Although the general standard of living has increased, widespread poverty still exists in rural areas and some basic freedoms continue to be suppressed.

Lessons from Adam Smith

In 1776, Adam Smith published An Inquiry into the Nature and Causes of the Wealth of Nations. *Written to "instruct" governments in the policies they should implement,* The Wealth of Nations *stated that society had a moral obligation to see to it that everyone, especially the workers, had a decent standard of living. Smith's conclusion was that this could be achieved only through a free-market system; by "free," he meant that people should be free to buy and sell goods and services in a system established by government.[3] This conclusion was based on two insights: first, that competition would lead to the most effective creation of wealth; and second, that effective competition depended on government regulation. These insights still hold true today.*

In Smith's day, however, the government was not seeing to it that there was effective competition. In fact, at the urging of businesses, governments protected industries from competition by imposing tariffs on imports, as well as employing other barriers, such as import quotas. Such restrictions persist today. Adam Smith had observed that businesses would try to short-circuit competition by convincing the government that it was in the national interest to protect them from competition. This had two negative effects: first, purchasing power, especially of low-income wage earners, was reduced; and second, companies would not be interested in innovation if they could make satisfactory profits without the extra effort of improving their performance or innovating.

Smith also noted that companies often formed associations that put pressure on the government to pass legislation that would give them a competitive advantage in the marketplace. They often also colluded to raise prices all at the same time or to reduce output below demand so that they could raise prices. It was the task of government to withstand these pressures from business and to stop collusion that artificially raised prices. This pressure on government to distort competition was not limited to companies, but was also exerted by professional organizations and craftsmen who were members of guilds. Smith was not against such associations per se, but warned governments that they were not interested in the well-being of the public but rather of themselves. He said, "Whenever people or businesses can promote their self-interest at the costs of the public at large they will."

Smith recognized this self-interest as the "invisible hand":

> *By preferring the support of domestic to that of for-eign industry, [every individual] intends only his*

> *own security; and by directing that industry in such*
> *a manner as its produce may be of the greatest*
> *value, he intends only his own gain, and he is in*
> *this, as in many other cases, led by an* invisible
> *hand to promote an end which was no part of his*
> *intention. . . . It is not from the benevolence of the*
> *butcher, the brewer or the baker that we expect our*
> *dinner, but from their regard to their own interest.*[4]

The Dalai Lama recognizes the danger behind acting out
of mere self-interest.

Adam Smith refers to the development of moral sense as imagining oneself in the position of others. That is what we refer to as "exchanging self for others." Unfortunately, Adam Smith did not stress sufficiently the need of people to train in imagining themselves in the position of others. Even though he had a keen interest in and insight into moral issues, Smith believed that competition and regulation could lead to prosperity for all. But I believe that Right View and Right Conduct are also necessary. Without considering the impact of one's decisions on others, it is not possible for regulation and competition alone to result in a decent standard of living for all.

Adam Smith and other economists have concerned themselves with the generation of wealth, but they do not provide any guidance on the distribution of wealth. Karl Marx, on the other hand, looked at this the other way around. He was only interested in the distribution of wealth, not in how to generate it. In my view, both the proper creation of wealth and the proper distribution of it are very important. In order to reach such goals, one requires the right policies and the application of Right View and Right Conduct.

> *In many respects, Adam Smith was ahead of his time. He knew that government had many tasks, among them the development of physical infrastructure, the establishment of property rights, and an effective system of justice, topics that we have addressed in chapter 8. Property rights he deemed very important because they make it attractive for people to invest, save, and improve their standard of living. Only under these conditions can there be a truly free market that encourages fair distribution of wealth for all.*
>
> *Another of Smith's concerns, much like the Dalai Lama's, was the idea that people would start to believe that ever-increasing wealth would make them happy. He wrote that even though there was the potential for that misunderstanding, the pursuit of wealth at least helped to solve the problem of poverty. This optimism carried over to other things. Smith believed that it is part of human nature to be pleased when others are happy, even though one gains no benefit from it. He also wrote that moral people do not seek approval but self-approval that they have lived up to proper moral standards, even when their actions go unrecognized. He lived that way himself: when he died, he left his substantial savings to charitable causes.*

With Freedom Comes Responsibility

Friedrich von Hayek, a well-known twentieth-century economist and proponent of free-market capitalism, recognized that establishing and protecting freedom and liberty in a free-market system is a major challenge. He wrote:

> *Freedom and responsibility are inseparable. Many people fear freedom. It is doubtless because the opportunity to build one's own life means an unceasing task, a discipline that man must impose upon himself if he is to achieve his aims. We assign responsibility to a man not in order to say that he might have acted differently, but in order to make him act differently in the future. If I have caused harm to somebody by negligence or forgetfulness, this does not exempt me from responsibility. It should impress upon me more strongly than before the necessity of keeping such consequences in mind. A free society probably demands more than any other that people be guided in their action by a sense of responsibility which extends beyond the duties exacted by the law.[5]*

The free-market system, as we know, fosters a high level of average income but still unacceptable levels of poverty. Because of this, Hayek considered it the responsibility of those working within a free-market system to take care of the poor. He wrote:

There can be no doubt that some minimum of food,
shelter and clothing, sufficient to preserve health,
and the capacity to work as well as education, can
be assured to everybody without endangering free-
dom in a society that has reached a general level of
wealth as ours. [6]

The Dalai Lama recognizes this shortcoming of most free-
market economies and supports a compassionate approach
in what he calls a responsible free-market economy.

Even though Adam Smith was concerned with the moral di-
mensions of the economic system, many of his successors ignored that aspect. I consider an economic system without a
moral dimension to be dangerous. That is why I want to add the
dimension of "responsibility" to "free market." I agree with the
concept of freedom advocated by Smith and Hayek but feel it
does not take us far enough.

Responsible behavior is necessary because of the limitations
of what can be achieved by laws and regulations. It is impossible
for governments to make people behave decently by law. The
system will work well only when the leaders of businesses and
government have the right motivation and act accordingly. With
every action, people should ask themselves: Am I acting responsibly? This may sound rather obvious to many people, but everybody can point to a lot of irresponsible behavior around them
from others while not recognizing their own irresponsible behavior. And even if they do, they are often too busy, lazy, or set in
their ways to take steps to remedy that behavior. And remember,
when people act responsibly they not only help improve life for

others, they will be much happier, because they will have peace of mind. They will feel that they have done the best they can—realized their full potential—which, as we saw in chapter 8, is the key to achieving true satisfaction in life.

Achieving Freedom and Prosperity for All

The goal of ensuring freedom and prosperity for everyone is, of course, a lofty one. Over and over in this book, we have encouraged leaders in business and government to take the initiative in addressing poverty, promoting environmental sustainability, protecting human rights and access to justice, making diversity a strength. It is the Dalai Lama's contention that if all these matters are actively being pursued, it will translate to greater peace and more widespread happiness for the global population. Here, the Dalai Lama sums up the possibilities and the promise in each of these areas, one by one.

The Reduction of Poverty

When traveling around the world, I have been both surprised and dismayed by the great prosperity in some parts and the abject poverty in others. The number of rich people in the world is growing, yet at the same time, the poor remain poor and in some cases are becoming even poorer. This I consider to be completely immoral and unjust.

As leaders, whether in business, in government, or in our communities, we need to address the issue of the gap between the rich and the poor, on both a global and a national level. The fact that some portions of the human community have abundance and others on the same planet are going hungry or even dying of starvation is not only morally wrong, but is also a source of unrest.[7]

A Sustainable Economy

The concept of interdependence is at the heart of environmental sustainability, for interdependence is a fundamental law of nature. The myriad forms of life on this planet—from the oceans to the forests to all species of flora and fauna that surround us—rely on interdependent patterns of energy, water, and air. Without the proper interaction, life dissolves and decays.

Today, as threats to our ecosystem become graver and graver, we need to appreciate this fact of nature far more than we have in the past. Our ignorance of these interdependent systems and the extent to which our actions disrupt them is directly responsible for many of the problems we face. We have to limit, as much as is feasible, our consumption of natural resources and move as fast as possible to sustainable development. Allowing unchecked population growth, in developed and undeveloped nations alike, will only put a further draw on our precious resources. And the fight over those resources is a serious threat to sustained peace. This is why it is critical that businesses and individuals alike respect the delicate matrix of life and allow it to replenish itself.[8]

The Protection of Human Rights

All human beings, whatever their cultural or historical background, suffer when they are intimidated, imprisoned, or tortured. It is not enough to define human rights as the United Nations has done; they must also be implemented. Rights depend on responsible action. This is why I put so much emphasis on the word "responsible" when I advocate responsible free-market economy.

Some Asian governments that are now participating in the free-market economy have contended that the standards of human rights used by the West cannot be applied to Asia and other developing countries because of differences in culture. I do not share this view, and I am convinced that the majority of Asian people do not either, for it is the inherent nature of all human beings to yearn for freedom, equality, and dignity; and they have an equal right to achieve it. I do not see any contradiction between the need for economic development and the need to respect human rights, as long as these are linked to the obligation of responsible action.

Tradition can never justify violating human rights. Discriminating against people from a different race, against women, and against weaker sections of society may be traditions in some regions, but these behaviors are inconsistent with what should be a universally recognized standard of human rights, and they must change. This is why throughout the book I have stressed that businesses and business leaders must strive to promote equality and prosperity for all human beings.[9]

The Strength in Diversity

I believe that the rich diversity of cultures and religions should help to strengthen the vitality of communities and not be a source of conflict, as is the case in many parts of the world. While there are fundamental principles that bind us all as members of the same human family, regardless of race and religion and gender, I believe that the world's cultures are interdependent, each with something valuable to teach. This is why I consider diversity to be a very powerful, positive thing.[10]

We as Tibetans, for example, have a unique culture that contributes to society's larger store of ideas. One of our unique cultural features is the knowledge we have developed based on the teachings of Buddha. These teachings did not originate in Tibet but in India. That shows the value of the exchange of cultures and ideas. It enriches the mind. This is why, as I have stated, it is to the advantage of business leaders everywhere to foster cultural diversity in the workplace, their companies, and the global market. As Mahatma Gandhi said:

> I do not want my house to be walled in on all sides and my windows to be stuffed. I want the cultures of all lands to be blown about my house as freely as possible. But I refuse to be blown off my feet by any.[11]

A Call for Universal Responsibility

My ideas about universal responsibility have evolved from my studies as a Buddhist monk. As Buddhists, concern for the well-being of others compels us to reach out to all living beings. Too often, people's interest in the well-being of others is limited to their family and friends or those who are helpful to them. That is not enough. We should be concerned for the well-being of everyone universally. We can take strong action to defend ourselves against aggressive enemies, for example, but we should never forget that they are also human beings.[12]

Interdependence among countries has increased dramatically through economic integration, advancements in communication, and low-cost transportation. It has become very old-fashioned to think of social responsibility only in terms of "my nation" or "my country," let alone "my village." Today, businesses and governments have the responsibility not only to ensure the future happiness of their own people, but also to promote happiness and prosperity in other countries. I do not believe that we will achieve a borderless world anytime soon. However, I have been encouraged by developments, such as the European Union, that show that countries are learning to share some aspects of their national sovereignty. I hope that similar developments will occur in other regions. The United Nations is providing some important guidance, and useful action, at a global level. Nevertheless, its capabilities to solve the world's problems are still quite limited. I am in favor of an increase in those capabilities but of looking toward other solutions as well.

Freedom is precious. Freedom that leads to happiness depends on responsible actions by people as individuals and as leaders in organizations. Leadership that acknowledges universal responsibility is the real key to overcoming the world's problems, and to achieving personal success and happiness.

Epilogue

If you remember only two concepts after reading this book—Right View and Right Conduct—and keep these two principles vivid in your mind, your decision making will improve, as will your satisfaction with life. With Right View you will examine your intentions and make sure that you consider the consequences of your actions not only for yourself but also for your organization and the well-being of others, and will do your utmost to avoid causing harm. You will also be able to reduce the negative thoughts and emotions that lead to wrong decisions and unhappiness for yourself and others.

When you become a leader, your power to influence and your ability to get things done grow very substantially. With that boost in power comes an increase in your responsibility to make the right decisions. Making the right decisions in an interconnected world is becoming more challenging all the time. When you are able to keep a calm, collected, and concentrated mind even under intense pressure, you will be better able to reach the right

conclusions and consider the consequences from many perspectives—short-term and long-term, from the perspectives of
employees, customers, shareholders, and society at large.

Globalization is a positive development as long as leaders of
global corporations act responsibly and develop a holistic view
of their role in society. And since organizations are also dependent on governments to act in a responsible manner, businesses
should work constructively with governments to achieve a responsible free-market economy and reject an economic system
without moral values.

This book project began with a discussion about integrating
capitalism and Buddhism. By the end of the project, it had become very clear to me that investments are necessary to create
prosperity. Investments require capital. Satisfying the need for
capital is therefore very important. The problem with the word
"capitalism" was that it made me think of those irresponsible
capitalists who exploit workers, thereby becoming very rich
while the workers remain poor. This problem has not disappeared altogether, particularly in poor countries.

Capital is a means, not an end. The end is freedom and prosperity for all. This can best be reached by a free-market system
in which all participants act responsibly. In my way of thinking,
integrating capitalism and Buddhism happens when Right View
and Right Conduct become an integral part of the economic system. I see the word "responsible" in this context as standing for
Right View and Right Conduct and therefore hope that the
words "responsible free-market economy" will come to replace
the words "capitalist system."

Inequality in personal wealth is as old as civilized society.
With the scientific knowledge, technology, and understanding of

the mechanisms of wealth generation now available, achieving a decent standard of living for all has become definitely within reach. My hope is that the ideas presented in this book will inspire many leaders and organizations to work with patience and enthusiastic effort toward reaching that goal.

Acknowledgments

This book is the result of teamwork, and we would like to thank all those who participated.

In our meetings in Dharamsala, the two authors benefited from the constructive contributions of Tendzin Choegyal, the youngest brother of His Holiness the Dalai Lama; Tenzin Geyche Tethong, private secretary of His Holiness, former monk, and minister in the Tibetan government-in-exile; and Venerable Lhakdor, a monk who is head of the Tibetan Library in Dharamsala.

Jan Kalff (former CEO of ABN AMRO) and Folkert Schukken (former member of the board of management of SHV) in the Netherlands reviewed the many versions of all the chapters to make sure that the texts were helpful to businesspeople and contributed their own very extensive experience. Cor Herkströter (former CEO of Shell and chairman of the board of ING) shared his experience of developing and implementing business principles in global organizations, especially in Royal Dutch/Shell. Sir

Leonard Peach shared his experience from IBM and working with government.

Venerable P. A. Payutto from Thailand contributed with insights from Theravada Buddhism. Phra Ajahn Surasak Khamarangsi guided Laurens's retreat. Sirithorn Rutnin and Thitinart na Patalung organized additional practical guidance in the application of Buddhist principles.

Nicholas Brealey, our U.K. publisher, recognized the importance of the message in this book at an early stage. He played a vital role in structuring, sequencing, and concentrating the message to make the text accessible and interesting for a wide public. Our editor, Sally Lansdell, made the text flow and ensured that the different sections fitted logically together.

Without my son Jörgen this project would not have begun. He raised my interest in Tibet and in His Holiness the Dalai Lama. My wife, Maria-Pia, has had to put up with a husband who, once he gets into a subject, can think and talk about nothing else. That meant that when the subject was Adam Smith, she got Adam Smith for breakfast, lunch, dinner, and as a nightcap for several days until the next subject took over. To both my son and my wife, my thanks.

Notes

CHAPTER ONE

1. The image of the net of Indra is used under a Creative Commons license from http://commons.wikimedia.org/wiki/Image:Indrasnet.jpg.
2. Robert H. Rosen, *Just Enough Anxiety: The Hidden Driver of Business Success* (New York: Portfolio, 2008), p. 15.
3. The company is SHV Holdings NV, the largest privately owned company in the Netherlands, involved in energy, transport, consumer goods, and the provision of private equity.

CHAPTER TWO

1. Sherron Watkins, "Ken Lay Still Isn't Listening," *Time*, June 5, 2006.
2. His Holiness the Dalai Lama, *The Universe in a Single Atom: The Convergence of Science and Spirituality* (New York: Morgan Road Books, 2005), p. 177.

CHAPTER THREE

1. His Holiness the Dalai Lama, *Awakening the Mind, Lightening the Heart* (New York: HarperCollins, 1995), p. 56.

2. His Holiness the Dalai Lama, *Practicing Wisdom* (Boston: Wisdom Publications, 2005), p. 30.

3. His Holiness the Dalai Lama and Daniel Goleman, *Destructive Emotions: How Can We Overcome Them?* (New York: Bloomsbury, 2003).

4. Amanda Ripley, *The Unthinkable: Who Survives When Disaster Strikes—and Why* (New York: Random House, 2008).

5. Howard Cutler, "The Mindful Monk—Dalai Lama Interview," *Psychology Today,* May 2001.

6. His Holiness the Dalai Lama, *Transforming the Mind* (London: Thorsons, 2000), p. 8.

7. Thubten Yeshe, *The Tantric Path of Purification* (Somerville, Mass.: Wisdom Publications, 1995), p. 38.

8. Piet Hut, "Life as a Laboratory," in *Buddhism and Science: Breaking New Ground,* ed. B. Alan Wallace (New York: Columbia University Press, 2003).

9. His Holiness the Dalai Lama, *Cultivating a Daily Meditation* (New Delhi, India: Indraprastha Press, 1991), p. 110.

10. His Holiness the Dalai Lama, Lecture at Kalmuck Mongolian Buddhist Center, New Jersey, www.Circle-of-Light.com/Mantras.

CHAPTER FOUR

1. Chester I. Barnard, *Dilemmas of Leadership in the Democratic Process* (Princeton, N.J.: Princeton University, 1939).

2. Jim Collins, *Good to Great: Why Some Companies Make the Leap . . . and Others Don't* (New York: HarperBusiness, 2001).

3. Jack Welch and Suzy Welch, "State Your Business," The Welch Way, *Business Week,* January 3, 2008.

4. The Right Conduct examples come from Vodafone.

5. Barnard, *Dilemmas of Leadership.*

6. Lama Thubten Zopa Rinpoche is spiritual director of the Foundation for the Preservation of the Mahayana Tradition.

CHAPTER FIVE

1. Venerable P. A. Payutto, *Buddhist Economics: A Middle Way for the Market Place* (Badger, Calif.: Torchlight, 1996).

2. *Samyutta Nikaya*, I.89ff.

3. *Buddhist Economics*, chapter 4.

4. *Anguttara Nikaya*, I.12.

5. *Digha Nikaya*, 26; *Cakkavattisihanada Sutta;* and *Kutadanta Sutta*. See also Walpola Rahula, *What the Buddha Taught*, rev. ed. (Washington, D.C.: Atlantic Books, 2000).

6. Peter Senge, foreword to *The Living Company: Growth, Learning and Longevity in Business*, by Arie de Geus (London: Nicholas Brealey Publishing, 1999).

7. Arie de Geus, *The Living Company: Growth, Learning and Longevity in Business* (London: Nicholas Brealey Publishing, 1999), pp. 17–18.

8. United Nations, Universal Declaration of Human Rights, available at www.un.org/Overview/rights.html.

9. Abraham H. Maslow, *Motivation and Personality*, 3rd ed. (New York: HarperCollins, 1987).

10. *Dhammapadatthakatha*, III.262.

11. Fred Hirsch, *Social Limits to Growth* (London: Routledge & Kegan Paul, 1976).

12. Richard Layard, *Happiness: Lessons from a New Science* (New York: Penguin, 2005); Andrew Oswald, "How Much Do External Factors Affect Wellbeing? A Way to Use 'Happiness Economics' to Decide," *Psychologist* vol. 16, no. 3, 2003, 140–41; E. Diener and R. Biswas-Diener, *Rethinking Happiness: The Science of Psychological Wealth* (Blackwell, 2008); Martin Seligman, *Authentic Happiness* (London: Nicholas Brealey, 2003).

13. Bruno S. Frey and Alois Stutzer, *Happiness and Economics* (Princeton, N.J.: Princeton University Press, 2002).

14. Mark Honigsbaum, "On the Happy Trail," *Observer*, April 4, 2004.

15. Frey and Stutzer, *Happiness and Economics*.

16. Hammalawa Saddhatissa, *Buddhist Ethics* (London: Wisdom Publications, 1987), p. 128.

CHAPTER SIX

1. Bruce Murphy, "In a Generation, Gap Separating Compensation of Chiefs, Others Widens," *Milwaukee Journal Sentinel,* October 9, 2004, available at www.jsonline.com.

2. Geoff Colvin, "AmEx Gets CEO Pay Right," *Fortune,* January 21, 2008.

3. FTSE Group, *FTSE4Good Index Series Factsheet,* 2007.

4. Organisation for Economic Co-operation and Development, *Annual Report on the OECD Guidelines for Multinational Enterprises 2007,* available at www.oecd.org.

5. United Nations, *What Is the UN Global Compact?,* available at www.unglobalcompact.org/AboutTheGC/index.html.

6. McKinsey & Company, *Shaping the New Rules of Competition,* July 2007.

7. *2007 World's Most Ethical Companies,* available at http://ethisphere.com/2007-worlds-most-ethical-companies.

8. Fluor Corporation, press release, May 21, 2007.

9. *2007 World's Most Ethical Companies,* http://ethisphere.com/2007-worlds-most-ethical-companies.

10. Marc Gunther, "Money and Morals at GE," *Fortune,* November 15, 2004.

11. Tony Rice and Paula Owen, *Decommissioning the Brent Spar* (Oxford, U.K.: Routledge, 1999).

12. Royal Dutch/Shell, *Profits and Principles—Does There Have to Be a Choice?,* 1999.

13. James Smith, "Putting What We Learned from Brent Spar into Practice," *Greenpeace Business,* April 2005.

14. Rice and Owen, *Decommissioning the Brent Spar.*

CHAPTER SEVEN

1. Adapted from His Holiness the Dalai Lama, "Humanity and Globalization" (lecture, UNESCO, December 8, 1998).

2. United Nations Development Programme, *Human Development Report,* 2004.

3. Samuel Palmisano, "Multinationals Have Been Superseded," *Financial Times,* June 11, 2005.

4. IBM, "Global Procurement Policy Statement," available at www.ibm.com.

5. IBM, *Innovations in Corporate Responsibility, 2004–2005,* "Our People," p. 20.

6. Marc Gunther, "Money and Morals at GE," *Fortune,* November 15, 2004.

7. Aryn Baker, "Tulsi Tanti: Windpower Saved His First Factory. Now He Wants to Harness It to Help Save the World," *Time,* October 29, 2007; Rebecca Bream and Fiona Harvey, "Suzlon Plans to Double Wind Turbine Capacity," *Financial Times,* October 29, 2007; "Indian Firm Wins Wind Power Fight," BBC News, newsvote.bbc.co.uk.

8. Clay Chandler, "India's Firms Build Global Empires," *Fortune,* October 22, 2007.

9. Malcolm Doney, "Carbon Cutting," *Developments* (UK Department for International Development), issue 39, 2007.

10. Ibid.

CHAPTER EIGHT

1. Singh quotes here and following are from a PBS interview with Dr. Singh, June 2, 2001.

2. The originator of this idea was Hernando de Soto, founder and director of Peru's Institute for Liberty and Democracy. Hernando de Soto, *The Other Path: Invisible Revolution in the Third World* (New York: Basic Books, 1989); Hernando de Soto, *The Mystery of Capital* (New York: Basic Books, 2001).

3. World Bank, *World Development Report 2005,* p. 246.

4. World Bank, *Doing Business in 2004,* country tables.

5. Muhammad Yunus, "What Is Microcredit?," September 2007, www.grameen-info.org/bank/whatismicrocredit.htm.

6. Ibid.

7. Information on BRAC is drawn from www.brac.net/history.htm.

8. "International Committee of Religious Leaders for Voluntary Family Planning Calls on President Bush to Release $34 Million for UNFPA," *Progressive Newswire*, April 30, 2002.

9. His Holiness the Dalai Lama, Lecture, September 28, 1996, available at www.dalailama.com.

10. Figures and projections are from the Population Reference Bureau.

11. Unilever, Corporate Purpose Statement, available at www.unilever.com.

12. Unilever, "Helping Women, Creating Entrepreneurs," www.unilever.com.

13. *Financial Times*, December 7, 2005.

14. Information on this case study is drawn from Unilever, "Indonesia: Exploring the Links Between Wealth Creation and Poverty Reduction," available at www.unilever.com, and Jason Clay, "Exploring the Links Between International Business and Poverty Reduction: A Case Study of Unilever in Indonesia" (Oxfam GB/Norib Oxfam Netherlands/Unilever, 2005), available at www.oxfam.org.uk.

15. His Holiness the Dalai Lama, comments on Burma on a visit to Thailand, February 18, 1993.

16. Excerpted from His Holiness the Dalai Lama's acceptance speech at the Congressional Gold Medal Award Ceremony, October 18, 2007, available at www.dalailama.com/news.171.htm.

CHAPTER NINE

1. Adapted from a speech given by His Holiness the Dalai Lama on October 21, 2007, available at www.dalailama.com/news.174.htm.

2. Library of Congress Country Studies, *China and the Four Modernizations*, available at www.country-studies.com.

3. Adam Smith, *An Inquiry into the Nature and Causes of the Wealth of Nations* (Edinburgh, 1776).

4. Ibid., book 4, chapter 2.

5. Friedrich F. Hayek, *The Constitution of Liberty* (University of Chicago Press, 1960), p. 74.

6. Friedrich F. Hayek, *The Road to Serfdom* (University of Chicago Press, 1944), p. 124.

7. Adapted from a speech given by His Holiness the Dalai Lama, available at www.dalailama.com/page.45.htm.

8. Adapted from a speech given by His Holiness the Dalai Lama, available at www.dalailama.com/page.86.html.

9. Adapted from a speech given by His Holiness the Dalai Lama, available at www.cosmicharmony.com/Tibet/Dalai Lama/DalaiLama.htm.

10. Ibid.

11. Mohandas K. Gandhi, *All Men Are Brothers: Autobiographical Reflections,* ed. Krishna Kripalani (London: Continuum International, 1980), p. 142.

12. Adapted from a speech given by His Holiness the Dalai Lama in India, available at www.spiritsound.com/bhiksu.html.

Index